# JUDGE DREDD™

# JUDGE DREDD™

## THE MEGA-HISTORY

### COLIN M. JARMAN
### AND
### PETER ACTON

Lennard Publishing

First published in 1995 by
Lennard Publishing
a division of Lennard Associates Limited
Mackerye End, Harpenden
Hertfordshire AL5 5DR

A catalogue entry is available from the British Library

ISBN 1 85291 128 X

Front cover illustration by Mike McMahon
Back cover illustration by Gary Caldwell
Inside front and back cover illustrations by Colin MacNeil

Design by Paul Cooper Design
Editors: Roderick Brown and Chris Hawkes
Reproduction by Leaside Graphics
Printed and Bound in Great Britain by
Butler & Tanner, Frome and London

# CONTENTS

# FOREWORD

*The Mega-History of Judge Dredd without John Wagner would upset the judicial status quo and leave fans drokking all over the world!*

This was the nightmare scenario that we faced, two weeks before our deadline – John Wagner had refused to grant us an interview. In truth, he offered us five minutes of his time, but what can you ask a man...THE MAN, who created, deserted, then returned to write – for the next eighteen years – Judge Dredd...in three hundred seconds? Writing the definitive Dredd history with five minutes from Wagner would be like writing about the Great Wall of China with just a Lego brick to go on.

We soon learned that Wagner's Great Wall of silence was nothing personal, just typical of the writer's reluctance to discuss the past. Fortunately, we traced nearly everyone else associated with Dredd, and with few exceptions all were willing to give their penny-dreddful-worth. Over fifty editors, writers and artists were interviewed, resulting in enough relevant material to fill three books. Despite this excellent response, we were still without John Wagner, who had been directly involved in writing almost ninety per cent of all Dredd stories over eighteen years.

Without Wagner the writer, and with Dredd artists outnumbering all Dredd writers by almost ten to one, the book, by necessity, would have to follow an artistic slant. Our first idea – *The Art of Dredd* – was to chart the visual evolution of Judge Dredd from the expert viewpoint of the eighty or so artists who had drawn him.

BUT...in seeking merely to set the creation of Dredd in time, we opened up a veritable can of worms, which quickly transmuted itself into a nest of vipers. Having approached this book off the back of what had been considered, naively, a similar publication – *Roy of the Rovers: The Playing Years* – we soon realised just how different *Judge Dredd* and *2000 AD* were from traditional boys' comics. Very quickly the story behind *Judge Dredd* became too interesting and, ultimately, too important to be dismissed within the confines of an art-book.

Fuelled by the passion, the devotion and, after almost two decades, the undiminished anger still felt by many key people, we realised there was an untold story that needed telling. With the help of all concerned, coupled with varying degrees of recollection and memory lapses, the story of how Judge Dredd came into existence has been pieced together. To put the origins of the character (and comic) into context, it has been necessary to rediscover earlier comics and heroes, along with their conventions and their controversies.

Reflecting the socio-political world around him, in 1977, Judge Dredd was born into troubled times – a gross, domestic product of a turbulent decade. An era of Cold Wars and Hot-lines, of Action and nuclear reaction, of mice and Minute-men. *2000 AD* was a stitch in a time-bomb transplanted into the heart of an ailing British comic industry by typewriter terrorists, with Judge Dredd the lead violinist in an orchestra of violence. Pulling the strings of this violent backlash were two young co-writers – Wagner and Pat Mills, who radically revitalised boys' comics. Where Wagner had been a clam, Mills was the pearl in our oyster. It was his enthusiasm that inspired our change of direction from art-book to mega-history. Mills's passion was also shared by many other former Dredd creatives, and eventually the realisation that the true story needed telling finally persuaded John Wagner to break silence. The time (forty-five minutes to be exact) and comments he gave us proved as invaluable as the Rosetta Stone in deciphering the mythos of Judge Dredd. This is not to be seen as denigrating the valuable time and assistance given to us by the legions of others; but once this book has been fully digested, Wagner's importance will become obvious.

Since the book has undergone triple bypass and open-heart surgery to reach its present format, it is necessary to briefly explain our methodology...

> Chapters One to Four cover the pre-history of Dredd and *2000 AD*.
> Chapters Five to Twelve cover the creation and launch of Dredd.
> Chapters Thirteen to Eighteen cover the first eighty-five weeks of published Dredd.
> Chapters Nineteen to Thirty-Three cover the last sixteen years of published Dredd.

This may appear strongly biased toward the early years (or weeks to be more accurate) but this relatively short period is where the definitive Dredd was formed. The final sixteen years produced another dilemma: which of the nine hundred or so remaining stories to cover? The choices were made by referring to the men who know best: John Wagner and his last four editors – Steve MacManus, Richard Burton, Alan McKenzie and David Bishop (who between them cover the sixteen years in question). These famous five nominated their definitive Dredd stories and anecdotes, as well as their favourite artists and artwork. Along with our own choice of key 'event' episodes, the final chapters capture the essence of sixteen years in just 56 pages.

This process of culling stories and anecdotes was necessary, otherwise we'd still be talking to artists, editors and writers for the next eighteen years – such was the recollection and interest generated by this book from within Dredd's creative circle. For those whose personal contributions have not found their way into this book, Volume Two (...and Three) may well redress this unavoidable imbalance.

But first, we hope you enjoy reading Volume One...*The Untold Story!*

COLIN M. JARMAN and PETER ACTON - July 1995

# IN THE BEGINNING WAS THE WORD . . . AND THE WORD WAS DARE

"Judge Dredd is simply the most significant character in modern British comics. He's in the same league as Roy of the Rovers and Dan Dare."
*STEVE HOLLAND – JANUARY 1995*

"Eighteen years ago, nobody thought they had anything to say. It was just that Judge Dredd was a very good character to tell stories about. Every now and then, a comic character enters a country's mythology – Dredd may be one, there aren't very many – Dan Dare was one."
*ALAN GRANT – JANUARY 1995*

*Judge Dredd first appeared in public on 26 February 1977 in an advert in Prog 1 of 2000 AD, having been a very difficult year in development.*

*[Left] Dan Dare – Pilot of the Future. One of two specially commissioned murals completed by Frank Hampson for the Science Museum in 1977 – for a Childrens' Space Exhibition.*

Although this book is primarily about the creation, development and evolution of Judge Dredd, his roots can be traced back as far as post-war boys' comics. As will become clear, the character of Judge Dredd was as much a product of the changing face of the British comic industry, as he was a metaphor for the troubled and often violent social climate at the time of his creation.

Just as this book celebrates the first eighteen years of the life and times of Judge Dredd, it is vital to look back to 1950 and the debut of another major action comic figure – Dan Dare. It was this post-war **pilot of the future** that shaped the course of the British comic industry which would inexorably lead to a new, clear dawn of the **lawman of the future.**

Dan Dare's origins can be traced to imported American horror comics, which contained violent scenes that shocked the nation. In February 1949, the Reverend Marcus Morris wrote an article for the *Sunday Despatch* in which he attacked these imported comics: "Horror has crept into the British nursery. Morals of little girls in plaits and boys with marbles bulging in their pockets are being corrupted by a torrent of indecent coloured magazines that are flooding the bookstalls and newsagents." In his article, Morris also described a typical comic horror scene: "A character murders a group of six policemen with a machine gun, chortling '*Dis is fun*'."

Under the creative aegis of the Reverend Morris and writer/artist Frank Hampson, *Eagle* was the Hulton Press's moralistic British answer to the horror comics. Launched on 14 April 1950 [see below], with a print run of one million copies, *Eagle* was an injection of quality into the traditional ink-on-your-fingers boys' comics, or as Hampson more eloquently put it: "Into this scrapyard of rusty old bicycles I'm going to drive a Rolls-Royce."

Frank Hampson wrestled with the sort of editorial decision that his successors were to face some thirty years later: "The main challenge was to find something spectacular for the front cover. It was a toss-up between a cowboy story and a space adventure. The great thing about science-fiction is you can keep changing the venue; if things gets bogged down on Venus, there's still the rest of the universe to explore. The 1950s were a time of terrific technological development, so sci-fi was enjoying a boom. And anyway, there was no way I could draw horses."

The twenty-first-century exploits of Dan Dare, his belligerent bat-man Albert Fitzwilliam Digby and their arch-adversary the evil green Mekon paved the way forward for home-produced comics and quickly became a national institution, ruling the waves of British comics for over a quarter of a century. The readership of *Eagle* rarely dropped below 750,000 in its first ten years. In the ensuing decades, despite many attempts to keep the strip in touch with contemporary styles and space-age technology, Dan Dare remained locked in the amber of his 1950s origins.

On 3 May 1969, International Publishing Corporation (IPC) who now owned *Eagle*, merged the comic (and a reprinted and relettered Dan Dare) with their own *Lion*. This merger was seen by IPC staff writer Jack Adrian as Dan Dare's death-knell: "*Eagle* was dead anyway; all we did was chuck earth on the coffin. When *Lion* gobbled up the comic, circulation was down to 25,000."

Ironically, only a few months before man landed on the moon, the **pilot of the future** was simply no longer science-fiction. At much the same time that two men were taking giant leaps on the moon, two other young men were about to take their first small steps in creating a giant read for mankind.

# THE CAN-DO KIDS DID GREAT

Pat Mills and John Wagner first met, in Dundee, while working for comic giants D.C. Thomson, but Wagner recalls their ambitions were slightly different: "Pat always wanted to be a writer, but I went to DCT because I needed to get out of the house."

Wagner, who was born in Pennsylvania in 1949, came to Scotland as a thirteen-year-old and started work for Thomson six years later. He recollects the early editorial experience: "It was in a place called the Fiction Department, where you read incoming scripts and replied to writers. You would listen to *Woman's Hour* on the radio, write a report on it and send it round all the magazine editors."

Mills similarly recalls his own humble beginnings, north of the border: "I started at D.C. Thomson as a magazine journalist in general fiction and the guy who was head of the department was John Wagner. Fiction was like a clearing house. You started working on things like *Mills and Boon* and *People's Friend* stories, but they decided I was suited for a teenage girls' magazine called *Romeo* – I was told I wasn't trendy enough for *Jackie*.

"I worked on *Romeo*, until John joined me as chief-sub, and after a year, we discussed going freelance to make more money from the obvious riches to be made in comics."

With a ground-level working knowledge of comics and writing under his belt, Mills took a career decision: "I left Thomson after a year to go freelance. John helped a little bit in those early days and certainly supported me in the direction I was going. As I got more work, he came and joined me."

As Wagner confirms: "Pat left to go freelance and I eventually joined him to work from his garden shed. We did that for almost twelve months."

The freelancers attacked the children's comic market and wrote twenty-three scripts for various IPC stories. Of these, IPC bought twelve, which Wagner describes as "pretty good for people who didn't know if they were going to be able to make a living freelance. From this we had regular characters like 'Jack Pott' – the gambling kid, and 'Tomboy' [both for *Cor!* in 1971]. Real mindless stuff, but it was money."

Wagner also remembers the duo's first police story: "One of the first things we did when we left D.C. Thomson was 'Yellowknife of the Yard', about a Red Indian in Scotland Yard [see page opposite]. It was rejected by *Hotspur* (a Thomson comic), but we eventually sold it to IPC."

While the two were still writing in Scotland, their considerable output attracted the

"Pat Mills and John Wagner are by far and away the best scriptwriting editors in the business, so I gave them the space to be creative without any of the management and administrative hassles that have bedevilled the publishing industry since."

*JOHN SANDERS – JANUARY 1995*

*[Above] Part of the writers' early humour included putting their own names into the strip - a consistent feature of future scripts, as Wagner explains: " 'The Can-Do Kids', which appeared in* Lion *[in 1971], was quite good, actually. It had a lot of the kind of humour that goes into my work now."*

close attention of IPC management, as Mills explains: "I wrote a girls' story called 'Anne of a Thousand Tears' about a girl in the Irish potato famine, which impressed the hell out of John Purdie.

"Purdie had previously worked for D.C. Thomson, so he knew that John and I had something to offer. Working for Thomson in those days was a passport to success – like the Coldstream Guards. It opened many doors because their training gave you the best grounding in the world.

"Purdie made a special trip to Scotland to meet us, and he arrived looking incredibly well-dressed, driving a flash sports car and impressed the hell out of us poor writers – still working in my garden shed."

Purdie reported favourably on the two writers to his IPC Editorial Director, John Sanders, whose policy was plainly formed: "After many years working on youth titles, I wanted to drag IPC's outdated publishing practices and output screaming and kicking into the 1970s, to usher in a new wave of street-wise realism in comics."

Mills and Wagner had stayed busy during this period and wrote, amongst other titles: 'Partridge's Patch' for *Jet* and the girls' story 'School for Snobs' for *Tammy*, until they parted company. Wagner confessed to the need for a split: "Our partnership lasted nine months, and we decided it was time to split up before we came to the point of blows."

Mills also realised a need to move on: "We'd argue the whole time over titles, everything. We both had radically different styles and creative goals. My stories tend toward my psyche – loosely defined as 'paganism and alternative life-styles', if not a little darker than that. John's writing is romantic but not emotional, while I'm emotional but not romantic. That's horribly simplistic but it does reflect our different perspectives."

Wagner made the first move south to work on the IPC girls' comics, leaving his former partner to mull over a solo career: "After John had moved south, to edit *Sandy*, I found I wasn't happy with what I was writing. I was really suffering because the comics I worked on were shit. And I was having to write this shit – to pay off a mortgage, support a wife and two kids. I felt if I was closer to the editorial stage of things, maybe I could find out how I could better write the sort of shit that they wanted."

Mills continues the story: "I followed John down to IPC and started as a freelance sub-editor on girls' comics – *Jinty*, then *Tammy*, which gave me an insight into editorial techniques. The people we worked with became aware of a sense of energy around us, and a sense of a new direction.

"Although girls' comics were staggeringly popular, we quickly realised boys' comics were going downhill fast. The IPC boys' comic empire stank. It reeked of complacency, lethargy, old and stupid ideas. It was a kingdom of naff and needed shaking up. These people were shit scared of losing their protected fiefdoms, so we stormed straight into their world."

Someone who was more than happy to welcome this new breed of forward-thinking editor to IPC was John Sanders, who soon developed a healthy respect for Pat Mills in their quest for a common goal – to redefine the boys' comic industry. At first, Sanders found it very difficult to give Mills the freedom and control they both knew was required to revolutionise IPC comics.

The catalyst to Mills gaining this much needed editorial freedom came from an ironic source, D.C. Thomson – IPC's main comic rival and Mills's former employer.

# ACTION STATIONS

In September 1974, D.C. Thomson launched *Warlord* – a World War Two comic, with a more aggressive and realistic format than previously depicted. When this new comic proved a success, IPC knew they had to follow suit and Sanders was then able to play his trump card.

Going over the heads of older and established editors, Sanders brought in Mills to create IPC's answer to *Warlord*. He was rejoined by Wagner – who returned to London and a writing career after a year-long sabbatical back in Scotland where he'd worked on a series of lowly paid manual jobs: caretaker, labourer and three months on a dredger.

This new IPC comic was created by the two non-union freelancers in the strictest secrecy, to avoid upsetting the unions and Sanders remembers the reaction of his own staff: "Many of our editors had been with the company for forty years, some starting off as lift boys. I had staff who were still operating in the fustian 1950s using pre-war techniques, and were setting themselves against what was happening in the streets, on television and in the cinema. The biggest enemy they could think up for our young readers was the park-keeper who shouted at them to '*get off the grass!*'"

"Then a guy like Pat Mills comes along, a freelancer operating at the fringe. I knew I had to make special arrangements for this man – he was part of my plan to get IPC editorial thinking into the 1970s."

Mills backs up this stance against established staff: "Sanders decided to give John and I – both who had little experience in comics – the chance and freedom to do our own thing. It was kept a dark secret that we were producing a new comic – *Battle Picture Weekly*. We kept our office door locked, and if anyone asked what we were doing we said we were producing a braille comic for the blind.

"When our secret finally came out, we were ostracised by everyone in the office. They wanted us to fail badly, but this hate only served to fuel our determination to succeed. We were spurred on to make *Battle* work and we got a lot of creative energy from this anger."

For their war comic, Mills and Wagner co-wrote a number of strips including: 'D-Day Dawson', 'Rat Pack', 'Lofty's One Man Luftwaffe' and 'The Terror Behind the Bamboo Curtain'. With his freelance protégés causing a major internal haemorrhage, Sanders was able to fend off any hostile in-house disputes by revealing the successful sales figures for his new comic.

Wagner recalls one of their most popular *Battle Picture Weekly* strips: "Pat and I had spotted a Spanish artist, Carlos Ezquerra, in a D.C. Thomson comic [possibly *Wizard*] and brought him in to draw our 'Rat Pack' story." [See right] This artistic move would have a massive significance in the years to come.

Following the sales success of *Battle Picture Weekly*, Sanders commissioned Mills to create another action comic – simply called *Action*. It was this ultra-successful and ultra-violent comic that, in its short, yet highly controversial shelf-life, paved the way for Judge Dredd. A precursor of the trouble to follow was given in two of

"***Action*** was the first working class comic with working class heroes."
*STEVE MACMANUS* – ACTION: THE STORY OF A VIOLENT COMIC *(1990)*

"***Action*** was about difference...it wasn't about violence...it was about being different."
*PAT MILLS* – FEBRUARY 1995

*Launched on 14 February 1976, Action was given a big in-house build up by IPC in its brother war comic* Battle Picture Weekly.

the quickly discarded titles for this new comic – *Dr Martens* and *Boots*.

The revolutionary new comic was also heavily promoted in the more traditional IPC comic *Valiant*, with the tag-line:

*Something special...Something different...is going to happen.*
*Its name is ACTION...the New Boys' Paper of the Seventies!*

With his creative cohort Wagner tied up editing *Valiant*, the first thing Mills did was to appoint long-time IPC editor (from *Lion*), Geoff Kemp, to helm the new *Action* comic. Mills's second decision was not to base the new publication on a single theme, in the same way as *Battle Picture Weekly* was war-based. Mills wanted to have a number of different genres of story: sport, spies, as well as war.

A further aspect Mills had introduced to his own work – as both commissioning editor and writer – was storylines and characters inspired by current cinema, television and real-life events. For *Action*, this led him to create: 'Dredger' [a name possibly taken from Wagner's part-time job] – a tough cop based on *Dirty Harry*; 'The Running Man' based on *The Fugitive*; 'Blackjack' – a black boxing champion like Muhammad Ali and, revealing another facet of his own psyche – The Beast, in this case, a killer shark 'Hook Jaw' whose inspiration was a focal point for the comic. As Geoff Kemp remembers: "We were given just twelve weeks to create the new comic. At the time, the film *Jaws* had come out and it was pretty clear that people were rather enjoying seeing bits of bodies floating around in the water; and we were really thinking we could go much more violent than the comics had done before. There was still a very 1950s attitude towards this sort of thing."

Ignoring the out-dated, IPC old guard, Mills recruited a new wave of young writers: Wagner scripted early 'Blackjack' stories, later being replaced by Jack Adrian; Steve MacManus wrote both 'The Running Man' and 'Sport's Not For Losers' (a tough sports story); Gerry Finley Day scripted 'Hellman of Hammer Force' (a World War Two story seen from the Germans' point of view) and Ron Carpenter contributed both 'The Coffin Sub' (a World War Two naval strip) and 'Play Till You Drop' (a traditional football story).

As Kemp explains, Mills used these new writers to tap a source of fresh ideas rather than for their pure literary skills: "The fact was that a lot of them weren't very good as writers but at least they had a fresh attitude. Through their inept way of putting things over we managed to catch a style which was different to *Valiant* or *Tiger*."

*Action* sold a quarter of a million copies upon launch, and the sales figures gradually levelled out at, a still impressive and very profitable, 160,000 per week.

With the undoubted success and notoriety of his new comic, Mills did not rest on his laurels but sought to improve and increase the violent content. Out went Carpenter's two tame strips to be replaced by Tom Tully's more violent strips: 'Death Game 1999' (inspired by the film *Rollerball*) and 'Look Out For Lefty' (a less than traditional soccer story from the man who had been writing 'Roy of the Rovers' for many years).

These changes and new stories proved Mills's judgement right as sales bucked the traditional trend of a comic never recovering some of its lost launch readership, by rising to over 180,000.

This mix of violence and success did not go unnoticed in the press. John Sanders [who faced the wrath of the *Evening Standard* 23 February 1976 – see right] knew the twin success of Mills's two violent comics could be repeated: "*Action* had been the first successful excursion into realism. From its first issue, I was on the look out for a format...a character...that could repeat its enormous and violent success – legitimately."

Sanders did not have to wait long for someone in-house to light the blue-touch paper of creative thought.

## AARGH lives –but the blood is printed red

JOHN SANDERS - "Only paces behind TV."

# KELVIN TURNS UP THE HEAT

The inspiration for the new comic came from an unusual source – IPC competitions writer Kelvin Gosnell, who recalls "going down to Mills's office to talk about a competition in *Action*. But as I walked in the door, this ginger volcano erupts at me asking '*Can you write scripts? Can you write stories?*'

"I told him I had enjoyed writing as a kid – so he asked me what I was interested in. Aeroplanes were my obsession then and Pat got me to write a script for a story called 'Suicide Club'. This got me scripting as a freelance for Pat, who was always pushing his writers for inspiration.

"I was a great sci-fi fan, having read the old sci-fi classics along with more recent stuff like Philip K. Dick and Harlan Ellison. So I was delighted when I read in Alexander Walker's movie article in the *Evening Standard* that George Lucas was spending a lot of money on *Star Wars*. Walker forecast that sci-fi was going to be the name of the game in Hollywood."

The idea of a themed comic was not new, as Gosnell points out: "All comics were themed – *Battle Picture Weekly* was war, *Roy of the Rovers* was football, *Action* was, well, action, violence...everything – but no British science-fiction comics.

"I'd been to see Jack LeGrand [Head of the Boys' Comic Department] and his deputy Sid Bicknell to suggest that they commission a sci-fi comic. They told me that science-fiction was dead and it would never sell. Undeterred, and armed with Walker's article, I mentioned it to Pat Mills, who told me to put it in writing. I sent Pat a memo [see page opposite], who passed it on to John Purdie and the rest is history...

"When Pat Mills first mentioned the idea of a sci-fi comic to me, I didn't think it would work."
*JOHN WAGNER – NOVEMBER 1990*

"In 1976 I gave *2000 AD* its title, which when I look back is quite ironic. Normally a successful comic lasts ten to twelve years, so I joked at the time we should call it *2000 AD*, because it would be dead and buried by then."
*JOHN SANDERS – JANUARY 1995*

**SCIENCE FICTION COMIC PAPER**

I am convinced that there is a hole in the juvenile market which we are not covering. Whilst some of our comics do carry science fiction stories, none of them aim exclusively at the SF field.

Moreover, the standard of SF currently appearing in our papers does, I feel, rely too heavily on gimmicks . . . the story lines are not strong enough, or ingenious enough to appeal to the true SF fan latent in our readers.

Admittedly, SF has a very much specialist and minority appeal, but it is a growing field. Most bookshops now carry their own, exclusive SF section and the field is due to receive a sizeable boost in 1976 . . . we've already had *Rollerball*, and there are FIVE other major SF films in preparation.

I am sure therefore that we should be giving some thought to the preparation of an SF paper, right now . . . even if it planned to run only as long as the boom lasts: it must make money while riding the crest and could be used for a merge when it becomes uneconomic. Although, given the right mix, I am certain that it would stand a good chance of surviving much longer than the movie boom.

The type of stories I envisage are:

*SURVIVORS* – In which there has been some dreadful holocaust and the survivors of same struggle against the elements and their fellow humanity to preserve civilisation and bring the planet out of chaos.

*GALACTIC ADVENTURE* – Set many hundreds of years in the future. Our hero is a wrongly discredited Captain in the Galactic Patrol. He alone knows the dreadful truth of an impending alien invasion, and he alone can stop it. An ideal story to use all the gimmicks you can think of AND bring in good strong story lines.

*TIME TRAVEL* – The possibilities are endless, both visually and story-wise. The ingenious paradoxes which can be screwed out of any time travel adventure are fantastic.

Other possible themes are: telepathy, teleportation, the perennial kidnap, robots, intelligent animals, intelligent COMPUTERS even!

Funnily enough, I also think that at least one text story could be included and still appeal . . . we would have to aim for an older market than our current comics anyway, to grab the SF fan.

It might even be possible to obtain serialisation rights to material from some established authors . . . Asimov, Clarke and Bradbury for example have produced work admirably suitable for the younger reader.

In conclusion, if you think that this is a sound idea, I'm more than willing to go into greater depth in research and the production of some scripts and/or a dummy.

KELVIN GOSNELL 18.12.75

*[Above] Reproduced with the kind permission of Kelvin Gosnell is his epoch-making internal memo.*

*TRIVIA NOTE: Logan's Run was not too far removed from Judge Dredd's future environment. The central character in the film is Logan – a sandman – whose sole duty is to terminate illegal runners.*

"Within two or three weeks I was whisked out of my staff job as competitions hack to go over and work full-time alongside Pat."

Even Mills was initially wary of Gosnell's idea: "Sci-fi had been a dirty word for many years in comics. When I set up *Action*, I was refusing to even consider sci-fi stories, since I knew they wouldn't be successful. However, after *Action* had been launched, sci-fi movie blockbusters like *Star Wars* were still in the offing, so it was the logical time to launch a new sci-fi action comic.

"I felt such a theme would allow British comics to have large visuals and move into the future away from the restrictions of writing about the past. To move beyond the existing framework which had become a little tired and silly. At the same time Hollywood was gearing itself up for the big sci-fi boom. *Logan's Run* was one of the many early 1970s sci-fi films which influenced our thinking."

Faced with creating IPC's third action comic in under two years, Mills was keen to complete a personal hat-trick of successes: "I knew I needed every damn thing in the comic to make it a success. *Action* had taught me the value of publicity – good and bad, so I decided to bring back Dan Dare. I'd looked at the back issues of Dan Dare and found what was quite a magical story, and decided to revive him."

The relaunch of Dan Dare in *2000 AD* wasn't welcomed by some of the people Mills was working with, as art assistant Kevin O'Neill confesses: "The only *2000 AD* story I disliked was Dan Dare, which had been put in for middle-aged dads and newsagents, and to create some publicity over the new magazine. But no matter how many times we tried to improve Dare, it never worked."

[Left] The new-look Dan Dare in Prog 1 of 2000 AD, given the prime full-colour spread.

[Below] The ultra-violent Dredger – who would beget an equally violent near-namesake.

YOU'LL LEARN SOON ENOUGH. MEANWHILE, A LITTLE BEAUTY SLEEP!

There was one thing Mills was strongly against: "I didn't want *2000 AD* to follow in the same old house-style of existing publications like *Eagle* or *TV21*. I actually saw sci-fi as a vehicle for increased action and violence, and, more importantly for myself, a chance to explore the difficult idea and concept of the human archetype of The Beast. *2000 AD* was not a vertical progression from previous comics, more a retreat into a darker world, where you could get away with anything."

His experience on *Battle* and *Action* had taught Mills that readers demand a certain type of hero – "an adolescent alter ego of invulnerability". Mills was immensely disappointed and frustrated with this formulaic hero-worship and longed to break the mould, over the heads of his readership, if possible.

Although he'd bought some media publicity and readership loyalty by reviving Dan Dare, Mills knew deep down that, for his comic to succeed, he would have to find a brand new future hero who was markedly different from any that had gone before.

In *Action*, Dredger had filled this central role of law and disorder. For *2000 AD* Mills was looking to create the ultimate, violent persona.

# BETTER DREDD THAN IN-BRED

Pat Mills brought in John Wagner as his script adviser to search for new sci-fi stories, but it was reviving an old character that added a new twist to the convoluted story, as Mills relates: "At that time, a Dan Dare movie was in the works and its producer Paul DeSavery panicked at the idea that I was going to resurrect Dan Dare before him. In order to *control* Dan Dare, he felt he had to buy this new sci-fi comic off IPC and allow me to create it as an independent paper, free from in-house politics and practices. John Sanders was sold on the idea and asked me to put a formal proposal to the board."

This twist in the tale opened up the creative possibilities for Mills: "On the basis we were going independent, I told Wagner we were finally in full editorial control of our own comic and could expect a fair share of the profits. This was one of the first stages

"Whatever its beginnings were, I always thought the idea of Judge Dredd was a very good one. He comes across as this psychopathic Nazi and he went absolutely against every political stance I have ever held, but I still loved it."
*JACK ADRIAN – FEBRUARY 1995*

of the royalty battle that took us another ten years to win."

Independence meant Mills could fully explore the dark side of his imagination and he knew where to start: "I'd been very taken by a *Comix* character called Mannix. This guy was a total bastard – a cop who would shoot people in the back and say '*Somebody's got to do this job...I'm the law!*' So, I said to John it would be lovely to have our own character of this sort."

Wagner went away to develop this violent cop character, and Mills, having been given license to fill the pages of *2000 AD*, developed his own stories, one being an occult horror story titled 'Hanging Judge'. The basic plot concerned an eerie guy – Britain's last hanging judge – who, along with a young companion, comes across illegal black magic practices being carried out at a place like Stonehenge. The judge recognises the man at the centre of the ritual as someone he had previously sentenced to death.

Since Mills knew "the readers want their comic characters to have a powerful status name", he named his creation Judge Dread, but he found this only partially excited his co-writer: "Wagner felt this hanging judge – *a sort of Dr Who of the occult* – was not right for the new comic. But he liked the name and asked if he could use it for his own story about the future cop who shoots people who drop litter."

Once again, Kelvin Gosnell provided a spark of imagination: "The name came from a Dennis Wheatley-type supernatural story that Mills had written under the name Dread, which John wanted to use for his own story. I suggested that they change the name to Dredd."

As far as Wagner was concerned there was no difficulty how the name was spelt: "Originally I was spelling it Dread – the name was just a bloody good name. I just saw Dredd as a hard-hearted white fascist!"

As for the original Hanging Judge story, the only trace is a brief entry in the *2000 AD Make-Up Book Prog 1-44* which relates to a four-page Mills script (for which he was paid £30) called 'Black Magic: Judge Dread – Original Instalment One' and was drawn by Argentine artist Horacio Lalia. A pencilled entry reads *Unsuitable – maybe except in Annual*. As far as Mills can remember the strip was never published – anywhere.

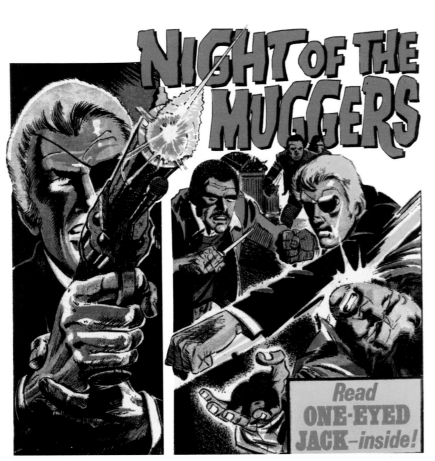

Wagner was happy that his cop character had a good solid name but was not so pleased with the direction his creation would go: "The idea for Dredd's name came from Pat, but I was responsible for developing the overall character – though he hasn't quite gone the way I'd envisaged. Originally, he was supposed to be Judge, Jury *and* Executioner. A man with that much power appeals to the bad guy in everyone – and believe me, it's there in everyone, even if it's buried deeply."

For his *new* character, Wagner again drew on a previous creation to inspire him: "Dredd came from an idea I had done in *Valiant* – 'One-Eyed Jack', which had some roots in the *Dirty Harry* movies.

"When Pat was putting together *2000 AD*, we realised from the success of 'One-Eyed Jack' this was the kind of story the paper should have – a really hard, tough cop. Obviously he would have to be harder, tougher, and mow people down without compunction."

When Wagner's first draft script came in, it was nothing like his original conception, much to Mills dismay: "John's first Dredd script was laced with political undertones, talking about dealing with commies, which I didn't think at all appropriate. I hadn't got what I thought I was going to get – a manic, merciless cop who shoots litter-louts."

Beneath the politics, Wagner had given his first script the calm, callous feel of a supernatural born killer: "My idea in microcosm was summed up by a scene where Dredd's riding along the road towards the scene of a siege and there's a citizen in the road yelling, 'Here comes Judge Dredd! He'll sort it all!' The guy is jay-walking, so Dredd runs him over with his bike. The guy's lying there bleeding all over the street, and Dredd says 'Jaywalking's a serious offence, citizen. Tell you what – I'll be merciful, I'll give you ten seconds to make the kerb.' The poor citizen crawls for it, but too late. Dredd shoots him and goes along to deal with the next situation.

"So, that was the original essence of Dredd. Okay, he's been toned down, and quite rightly, but Dredd's still there – that nasty, rotten bastard you love to hate."

De Savery's proposed buy-out left Mills free from any in-house code of ethics, but he still felt some of Wagner's action sequences needed juicing up: "I changed the ending and added a scene where Dredd, risks his own life, to rescue a criminal from a burning car, just so he can shoot him legally. It was my reflection of the way I thought John had wanted the character to be. John had always talked about this guy being an extreme lunatic and I thought that's what we've got to have."

Mills did agree with Wagner on the principle of indiscriminate and illegitimate use of violence: "There's one thing I've learned in all my work in comics: people love a bastard. There's nothing better than a bastard for getting readers either loving or hating them. And in Judge Dredd it's the unique combination where they can love and hate."

But the halcyon days of independent creative freedom were about to end, to Mills's dismay: "In the middle of summer 1976, as John and I were looking forward to our own stories and our own comic making us really rich, the IPC board refused to sell out to us and DeSavery. The comic was to be kept strictly in-house."

This news came as a bolt from the blue for the co-writers, who'd been led to believe the deal was a done thing. With IPC pulling the rug from under his feet, Mills felt it best to stand aside: "We'd both been paid for our material and work, and since the big one wasn't happening we told Sanders that we weren't hanging around any longer. I was ready to go back as a freelance and John, I think, was editing *Valiant* at the time. John was so annoyed at IPC's decision not to sell out, he wanted to withdraw his original Dredd story.

"After a couple of days, Sanders phoned and asked me to continue with the new comic and I told him he already had my answer. So he offered me £250 a week to do it – and that was a lot of money back then."

Up to that point, Mills remembers surviving on script fees from the new comic (approximately £40 per script), subsidised by writing girls' comic stories: "Sanders made me an offer I couldn't refuse, although I didn't really want to go back to commuting, putting more strain on my family. But I had been living and breathing this thing, and the money offered was life-changing money, which, as it happened, it wasn't.

"The catch was of course that with all that money they offered me, the new sci-fi comic had not only to be good, it had to be really good. From there on, I became even more fussy, even more picky than before."

He may have been happy to accept the IPC deal, but Mills could not ignore Wagner's reaction: "At that stage, John wasn't happy and went through a period of rejecting the in-house comic because he felt he'd been let down by Sanders. He may even have become jealous, as I would if I'd been in his shoes, over this large sum of money I'd accepted to create what was going to have been *our* comic."

John Wagner's recollection of this whole matter is somewhat clouded by the passage of time: "Unless it's something I've forgotten, this is the first I've heard of a Paul DeSavery buy-out. I knew he had some involvement with the Dan Dare film – he certainly wasted a lot of our time.

"What little I can remember of that period is we'd been promised to be allowed to do *2000 AD* as a contracting out job (not in-house) and would have more than a writer's interest in it – a profit motive. Pat was the mover on it, he was the one IPC wanted to do it. He called me in to talk over lots of stories and we developed one or two of them. I had been involved for a few weeks, I'd done Dredd and put a lot of imagination and creativity into it – more than just the usual work for hire deal. But the IPC board turned it down after all the work had been done on it. I was jarred off by it and thought to hell with it. I won't be writing for it anymore – I'd had enough."

Wagner's reaction did not surprise his former writing partner Pat Mills: "John obviously felt bad about a number of things, and his only way of registering it was to walk away from it. So I was left thinking how do I make this violent Dredd thing happen."

*This violent Dredd thing* delighted John Sanders, who, under pressure from his board over the unacceptable violence in Mills's previous comic creation, found Dredd's *legalised violence* irresistible: "*Action* had been staggeringly popular and the more successful it was, the worse the media outcry. The trouble was fuelled by those do-gooding consumer pressure groups, who only exist to get their own faces on TV and their own names in the papers. The easiest way to achieve this was to claim that the children of the country were being abused – and comics have always been an easy target."

John Wagner's own thoughts confirm this internal fanning of the flames: "In the early days, this level of violence wasn't discouraged. When *Action* came out, John Sanders positively encouraged it...until things went wrong."

Sanders stood by his own actions, and admitted that: "Wagner's Dredd character allowed us to get round the charge of *gratuitous violence* by having an officer of the law inflict the violence – in the name of the law. This was a Wagnerian master-stroke that Mills built on brilliantly and our enemies couldn't answer.

"The lawman was the obvious choice and solution. So much so, that we were able to do some really diabolical things which we couldn't have got away with in *Action*. With the *law* on our side we were able to hit back at our critics.

"Dredd didn't solve all my problems. Some of my senior editors couldn't accept the idea of a *bent* cop – a reality which our school-age readers were all too aware of in normal life. I knew we had to produce a comic, with strong stories, that closely reflected current trends and issues but I'm sorry to say I lost a lot of senior staff over this matter."

Like Sanders, Mills was also excited by the legalised aspect of violence: "I could immediately relate to this shift in heroic viewpoint, and I had told Wagner '*Let's give the buggers* [readers] *what they deserve!*' For too long the comic heroes had been wimpy with non-stop mayhem.

"If you look at *Battle*, D-Day Dawson represented the generic, GI Joe, Action Man kind of character, which to my way of thinking is fundamentally flawed and very unhealthy. Despite creating Dawson, I despised the character and I've had a subconscious feud with the readers over him to this day.

"I saw Wagner's killing machine as the ultimate, omnipotent character. Dredd was going to be the adolescent reader's nightmare, a strict character of non-forgiveness, a severe, father-figure who was always right and always on top."

Having a good idea as to the characteristics of Wagner's killer cop creation, Mills set about commissioning initial sketches. He already had in mind the best artist to bring the creation to life. Enter another D.C. Thomson and *Battle Picture Weekly* alumnus – Carlos Ezquerra.

# A SLICE OF BROWN DREDD

Born in Zaragoza, Carlos Sanchez Ezquerra drew for British comics while still living in Spain, in the days when D.C. Thomson were looking to use European artists, not because they were better than their British counterparts, but because they were cheaper.

It was at D.C. Thomson that Mills and Wagner first came across Ezquerra's work, so when they both moved down to London, it was natural for Pat Mills to call on Ezquerra to work on IPC projects: "From the very beginning of *Battle*, John and I brought Carlos in to do our *Dirty Dozen*-inspired story 'Rat Pack'. His stuff was wonderfully cool and we knew immediately that this was what we were looking for. This is a hip artist, this is a guy whose artwork reflects the world we live in."

"I find the best way to create a totally new character is to let your mind run free – throw in everything you fancy, then mix and shake well. I was also really keen on building Dredd up from a favourite prototype of mine – the Spartan hero."

*CARLOS EZQUERRA – JANUARY 1995*

*[Left]* Battle Picture Weekly's *'Major Eazy' allowed Spanish artist Carlos Ezquerra to put the 'olé!' into violence.*

For Ezquerra, this was the break he needed: "In September 1972, I arrived in Britain to work for D.C. Thomson comics having already drawn for them while I was still living in Spain. A few years later, IPC asked me to work on *Battle Picture Weekly*, for which I drew 'Rat Pack' and 'Major Eazy' – one of my all-time favourite characters."

Ezquerra recalls the first step in drawing Dredd: "While I was working on *Battle Picture Weekly*, Pat asked me to do some visualisations for a new character he was creating for another comic. In the first character outline, Dredd was described as a person who had the functions of the police but who could also dispense justice on the spot – a man who was allowed to take the law into his own hands. Pat also told me he must be dressed in black and ride a motor-bike."

For the first outlines, Mills remembers "giving Carlos a picture of Frankenstein from the 1975 movie *Death Race 2000* as the main reference for the Dredd uniform. It was a close-up pic of a helmeted David Carradine driving straight at the camera. I was convinced this image was the dog's bollocks.

"The characters are from much the same genre and I told Carlos this is how we wanted our character to look. Being a creative guy, Carlos said he could do better than that and came up with this really freaky guy. He'd taken him a million miles further than the original reference."

Wagner clearly recollects what reference Ezquerra used: "There had been this *Death Race* film – all I'd seen of it was an advertising poster [see above], which I cut out a newspaper. It was a picture of a guy with a black helmet on and very little of his face showing. I sent it to Carlos and he came up with Dredd, which was far more elaborate than I'd ever imagined."

For this foreboding helmet-look, Ezquerra remembers combining "a basic motor-bike helmet with a fifteenth-century executioner's hood, but this looked too simple for a future-look. Since I felt the character was a true Spartan, I added elements from an ancient Greek warrior's helmet to give Dredd's helmet that distinctly rounded, full-face look."

In his early Dredd visual, Ezquerra took one far-reaching decision on his own: "I covered up his face...for the simple reason that, if he was a Judge, he would have many enemies and these people wouldn't know what he looked like. So when he was off-duty (without his helmet) he could pass unnoticed and go about without being recognised."

Never seeing his whole face is an element of Dredd's character that has been perpetually retained, under punishment of death to any dissenting artist, which John Sanders strongly agrees with: "It was a tremendous idea of Carlos's not to show Dredd's eyes and hide them behind that visor."

But, Ezquerra knew he had to base what little was seen of Dredd's face on something: "When I first started to draw Dredd's *face*, he was based a little bit on Sylvester Stallone [whose movie *Rocky* had been released around that time in the summer of 1976]. I felt that Judge Dredd would be a man of few words and Stallone's Rocky Balboa was a good contemporary model. I also decided to give him some large lips – to put a mystery as to his racial background."

With the helmet and face complete, Ezquerra moved on to design the distinctive uniform that has barely changed in eighteen years. "Being a bike-rider, I decided he would need protection on the shoulders, knees and elbows – but in order to make him stand-out in the crowd, I made these pads much larger, almost too large to walk properly. I also added a chain to Dredd's badge to make him look tougher."

Dredd's original hand-weapon was an idea based on a New York cop's night-stick, but was soon discarded in favour of a more potent weapon – the LawGiver [see below].

Ezquerra's inspiration for Dredd's gun "was based on a 1908 German Navy Luger [see right]. Since I'd been used to drawing all sorts of World War Two guns for *Battle Picture Weekly*, I let my imagination run wild and came up with the gun of the future – based on a gun from the past. I wanted it to be a big, long handgun, something that got noticed and instantly commanded respect. To give the gun some extra body, I gave it a large magazine underneath the barrel, which makes it look much more powerful and persuasive.

Some of Ezquerra's designs and innovations came from his vivid imagination, others were purely logistical: "Putting Dredd on a bike posed a problem as to where to put the holster for his gun. When he was riding around, having it on his waist, cowboy-style, would make it difficult for a fast-draw. So I came up with the idea of putting the holster on the top of his right boot – which worked wonderfully, both technically and visually, as the gun is clearly visible and not tucked away in his waistband."

Ezquerra also brought the same thought and detail to his first visual of Dredd's bike: "I took the basis of a Harley-Davidson chopper, crossed it with the big, flashy American police bikes of the time and originally converted that look into a futuristic hover-bike, as we did with most of the other forms of transport in the city. But I felt a hover-bike was too clean, too smooth and much too gentle for such a violent man. This Judge needed some power and strength to *jet* around the city – he needed wheels. And did I give him some wheels! They were more like aircraft tyres than road tyres.

"I understand that the movie people mocked up a real bike based upon my design and found they couldn't steer the bike because the front wheel [literally an aircraft tyre] was much too large! Still, it looked hot when I first drew it."

But Ezquerra wasn't finished with his design: "I later added a large Eagle emblem on Dredd's right shoulder pad. I chose an Eagle because it was the current symbol of the American police and I felt the symbol would still be in use in the future. But I based my Eagle design on a source closer to my roots than New York City. I was always fascinated by the eagle that appeared on Spanish coins minted under the Franco regime – particularly the 500 pesetas. It looked different enough from the traditional American design to make it look uniquely futuristic."

*Evolution of the Lawmaster bike. [Above right] An early Ezquerra visual. [Right] Ezquerra's 1992 version, which also shows off the large shoulder pad, the Lawgiver gun and Lawrod rifle.*

Ezquerra seemed pretty content with his first visualisations: "Dredd was so successful because he was a little ahead of his time, particularly in the fashion sense. I drew him before the 1977 punk boom of black leather and chains, and well before the heavy metal movement, which he typified. I have always believed that successive generations went to the opposite extreme of its predecessor. In this case I thought the peace-loving, flower-wearing hippies would be superseded by a spiteful, black anarchic generation. *The Dredd generation!*"

The artist's enthusiasm for the new character was shared by his editor, as art director Doug Church confirms: "When Pat Mills first saw Ezquerra's sketches of this surly bloke sitting on a massive motor-cycle – he was orgasmic!"

Mills was so delighted he wanted to share this new creation with the whole world: "I even showed my mother, who said '*You guys are going to have one of the most successful characters of all-time*' – and this was a middle-aged, middle-class woman!"

From Ezquerra's preliminary sketches, Mills knew he had a major (soon to be mega) hit on his hands, and nearly everyone in the IPC offices was extremely excited about the new look. The one dissenting voice, however, was Dredd's creator, as Kevin O'Neill [then, art assistant] elaborates: "When John

Wagner first saw Carlos's initial character sketches of Dredd, he wasn't at all enamoured...'*Fucking hell! He looks like a fucking Spanish pirate! I'm not writing him, he looks fucking stupid!*'"

Wagner may also have been upset at the fact that Ezquerra's sketches were of a different age, as Mills remembers: "John's original image was of the very near future, say 2010, but Carlos went against this. His Dredd uniform was much more extravagant than Wagner had imagined and Carlos took him by surprise."

Almost twenty years later, John Wagner remembers his impressions of Carlos's early visuals: "I was unhappy with them, I thought they were way over the top. I was looking for somebody with much cleaner lines. I saw Dredd more like smooth glistening metal rather than Carlos's baroque Judge. But he was obviously right – it's a look that has lasted. Carlos is a great character creator; he was right and I was wrong."

Despite Wagner's initial reservations, Mills was always looking to expand fully upon an innovative idea, however far-reaching in originality, and was determined to stick with Ezquerra's visuals: "I was very comfortable with Carlos's uniform design, but I knew it could not possibly have been worn by a lawman of forty years in the future – this caused me a problem that took some fixing."

Carlos's initial drawings were sufficient however for Mills to give him the task of bringing a script to life.

# COMIC STRIPPED BARE

With the ultra-violence Mills had rewritten into Wagner's already over-the-top first script taking it well beyond the realms of acceptability by IPC, things didn't go any smoother for Mills and Wagner in developing their second. As Mills explains: "To safeguard them from criticism, IPC wanted the story to be set in a galaxy far, far away from Earth, but I insisted it be set in New York. John wanted it set in the near future.

"After the first *commie-burning finale* story, which was obviously extremely violent and nasty, came the second version written by John, after he walked out following the buy-out collapse. At this stage, there was the possibility of getting John back interested and involved."

Although Mills found Wagner's second story more acceptable than the first politically undertoned version, he still made a key change to Wagner's story by adding a deeper criminal element.

Once the two writers had agreed on a finished script, Ezquerra was given the task of drawing the first Dredd strip and he approached the script with a few ideas already clear in his own mind: "My impression of Dredd was that he was extremely violent and since he was patrolling a huge city full of lawless citizens, he would have to be lawless to have any effect. It was a case of everyone being lawless – but he was on the right side of the law, they were on the wrong side. It had the feel of a spaghetti western about it – but set many years in the future. I'd always imagined Dredd to be a very stern person for whom the law was everything and all personal feelings were suppressed – almost like a robot."

When Mills and Wagner wrote their second script [here referred to as BANK RAID], they knew the first published story would be the guiding light by which all subsequent stories would be led and, fittingly in Dredd's case, judged. The same could be said for Ezquerra's artwork – all future visuals would come back to his first strip.

By looking beneath the surface of the first four-page strip it is possible to ascertain what the threesome worked on and hoped to bring to the story. The whole story is reprinted – as it was originally drawn (except for three editorial changes to Ezquerra's artwork – see the illustrations and captions on pages 28 and 29).

"The first published story would always define all prior requisites of the Dredd character and it was crucial to get it absolutely right. If first impressions were wrong, the story and the character would suffer to the end of time."

*PAT MILLS – JANUARY 1995*

# JUDGE DREDD

MEGA-CITY LAW CONTROL TO JUDGE DREDD + BANK RAID IN NEW MANHATTAN + STREET LEVEL 95 + LAWBREAKERS ABOUT TO ESCAPE

*NO ONE CAN ESCAPE JUSTICE!*

2000

THRILL

SCRIPT WAGNER / MILLS
ART CARLOS S EZQUERRA
LETTERING B. NUTALL

*TRIVIA NOTE: The opening ticker-tape message was added at a much later date to the original strip (as were some additional explanatory captions).*

In critically dissecting the strip, the first point to make is that there is no year specified. The action is set in the future but exactly how far...ten years...a hundred years?

The opening spread is dominated by the title character, sitting astride his big, black, fat-tyred bike, smashing through what turns out to be the plate glass window of a bank. No subtle opening...and neither was subtlety lavished on Dredd's first words: *"No one can escape justice!"* Nothing out of the ordinary on page one – a man on his bike with a curt line in clichéd understatement – in what was planned as the central figure in an explosive new sci-fi comic.

And don't turn to page two [see right] in search of originality. This Judge isn't respected – he is there to be *smoked*. But, the dialogue and action bear an uncanny resemblance to a scene from 'One-Eyed Jack', a strip Wagner had written a few months earlier for *Valiant and Vulcan*. [See below right]

The first hint of any originality, for the reader, comes when Dredd pulls his gun from a boot-holster, as he dismounts from his stationary bike. Despite being *armed with a special gun loaded with six kinds of shell*, Dredd decides to make his presence felt using bovver-boy tactics reminiscent of *Action*'s football hooligan and juvenile crime stories. Ambivalently, Dredd dresses like a heavy-metal punk but acts like a contemporary skinhead.

Dredd's *stamp it out* pun encapsulates the writers' trademark humour. This quasi-comic device emulates the humorous asides perfected in the early Connery/Bond films – as an attempt to play down the level of screen violence, a gimmick freely imitated by Mills and Wagner, and still used in today's action movies.

Having "stamped" his authority on the first criminal, Dredd turns his attention and his gun to the next three in line, whom he dispatches with little effort or retaliation.

In this final frame on page two, Ezquerra is given the chance to reveal close-up detail of Dredd's helmet, lower face (with Ezquerra's trademark down-turned mouth and big lips), as well as the large eagle shoulder pad. During the ten occasions that Dredd actually makes an appearance in the strip, his distinctive eagle shoulder pad is only clearly detailed twice.

For the other eight times, Ezquerra has cannily managed to obscure this intricate piece of padding behind Dredd's gun or keep it out of our view altogether.

In more visible cases, the proud eagle appears to no more than a semi-amorphous lump. It is this technique that enabled Ezquerra to produce artwork fast and efficiently, albeit poorly detailed in places.

At the top of page three of the strip [see below left], a close up of the *special gun* is clumsily explained away by Dredd through tight-lips. Strangely, the other characters speak open-mouthed, whereas Dredd's lips seem glued together. A throwback to Ezquerra's idea to base the face on Rocky Balboa – not renowned for his crystal clear enunciation.

Overwhelmed by Dredd's awesome firepower, the rest of the gang try in vain to escape this one-man wrecking crew but quickly give themselves up. An exceedingly foolish decision, if they are fully cognizant of a Judge's autonomous powers of execution: "*There is no surrender. Onto the sidewalk where I shall carry out sentence.*"

It is indicative of Wagner's intended fascistic storyline that Dredd turns the executions into an exhibition, in front of cheering citizens. Such a cold-blooded dispensation of justice harks back to the public hangings at Tyburn and even to another eponymously named Judge – Jeffreys and his seventeenth-century Bloody Assizes.

At the top of page four [see above right], with the bank raid thwarted and executions carried out, Dredd reacts calmly to the crowds' almost riotous delight, by assuring them: "*I take no pleasure in terminating law-breakers*" and proceeds to sentence a cheerleading citizen to four hundred days for jay-walking. A harsh penalty for a petty crime – again setting the tone for the period, the Judge and his unquestionable powers of arrest, sentencing and execution. It is in these frames with the jay-walker that there is any of the true essence of Dredd's personality as he is known today: the tough, no-nonsense disciplinarian serving surprisingly severe sentences on extremes of justice. Murder and jay-walking are treated with the same emotionless formality by the lawman in black.

As foolish as the bank robbers, who had surrendered, the jay-walker tries to bribe the Judge, which Dredd dismisses as "*an odious offence!*" and, hardly moving a muscle, puts an end to the jay-walker's escape with another of his special bullets.

Finally, Dredd hands over to a comical-looking policeman in a scene which has all the gravity of the Special Patrol Group handing back control to Dixon of Dock Green. The Judge is young, sleek and athletic, the policeman is older, overweight, and appears slow, almost bumbling – possibly a futuristic incarnation of PC Bumble from Mills and Wagner's 'Yellowknife' strip for *Valiant* and *TV21* [page 11].

Despite seeing that justice has been served, the reader is left with the overpowering feeling that this Judge hasn't been tested. He did kill seven criminals, but it was with the consummate ease and lack of compunction of a part-time parish council rat-catcher. The villains are just not villainous, they appear so inept they actually give villainy a bad name.

Dredd's own character is reasonably well-defined as a cold, calm, coolly calculating city custodian. His actions are not excessive, he uses the minimum of effort to achieve results, he simply stands and delivers – his brand of justice. Without a foe of equal or greater abilities, he is totally wasted here as a comic strip hero.

The one spark of originality – Ezquerra's boot-holster – even turns out to be a gross miscalculation. It is fine when Dredd is seated on his bike, but becomes a life-threatening liability when standing upright. The extra time it takes to bend down and draw the gun from his boot, rather than his waist, suggests that he should have been equipped with more than one handgun.

This was one major flaw in Dredd's uniform that the film-makers had to make adjustments for, placing the holster on Dredd's thigh.

Overall, the storyline is flat, the plot is mundane and the action barely shifts out of first gear. Stripped down to basics, the story is nothing more than a futuristic variation of a Wild West sheriff, with his faithful horse, badge and shining six-gun, cleaning up Dodge City. Luckily for all concerned this strip got buried in the comic-strip equivalent of Boot Hill – without a headstone, until it was disinterred four years later.

As a piece of Dredd history, the strip is priceless...as the first Dredd story it is best remembered as a priceless piece of Dredd history.

[Below] In the original, the lawbreaker Dredd kicks in the face falls onto the flame-thrower who is standing right next to him. In the reprint, the flame-thrower has been completely excised.

Soon after IPC management had seen Ezquerra's four-page strip they rendered it unpublishable. Their judgement is revealed in the *2000 AD Make-Up Book Prog 1-44*: "...First four pages censored. Last page [Mega-City Poster] used in Prog 3 as Futuregraph." Ezquerra's evocative and imaginative four-page strip was deemed too violent, especially in the days when IPC were fending off flak from the media on the violent content of *Action*.

This aspect of violence is confirmed by Kevin O'Neill: "Carlos's strip was terrific and incredible, but it had to be changed because it was too violent. We all knew it was powerful enough to be a huge hit, but we know it would be extremely difficult to sell Dredd to the IPC board."

Even Wagner was forced to agree with IPC's ruling: "Originally Dredd did have the right to execute anyone he liked and that was one of the excesses [notably the roadside execution] that IPC decided to curb [sic]. I think they were probably right. A character like the original Dredd was just too unsympathetic."

For reasons of extreme violence the first Dredd strip did not see the light of day until it was reprinted in the *1981 Judge Dredd Annual*. Even then, some four years later, three major censorship changes were still made, as shown by the three frames from the original artwork.

[Above] In the original, Dredd's "dodgem" bullet originally went through two of the lawbreakers - killing them. In the reprint, the bullet has been redrawn to miss everyone.

[Right] In the original, when Dredd shoots the jay-walker in the back, there is evidence of the bullet hitting its target. In the reprint, this small detail has been taken out.

Looking at the overall impact of the strip, it is surprising that Mills and Wagner put this script into Ezquerra's hands. With such limited scope for action, thrills and character development, the artist achieved a noteworthy effort. In one key area, Ezquerra single-handedly redefined Dredd's world, and consequently the whole of the character's future development.

# POST-SCRIPT

When Mills saw Ezquerra's artwork for the BANK RAID script, apart from the immense thrill of seeing his joint creation fleshed out, he was impressed by two pencil backgrounds of a future New York City. The two frames that caught Mills's expert eye for detail being the execution scene and where Dredd first addresses the jay-walker.

Looking for further inspiration to improve and develop Dredd's environment, Mills asked Ezquerra to draw a full-page colour poster-pic of his vision of New York's future city-scape. And Ezquerra promptly obliged. [See page opposite]

Mills was so pleased with Ezquerra's imaginative city-scape, he took the artwork to a less than enthusiastic Doug Church: "Pat came to me with Ezquerra's full-page depiction of New York in Dredd's time. Pat was in raptures over it – but I thought it was a horrible piece of art, but he wanted to feature it as a full-page colour poster."

Although Church was not keen on Ezquerra's work, something in it sparked a momentous reaction: "The sheer immensity of the city struck a chord with a feature I had recently read in *Life* magazine, depicting the USA taken by infra-red photography from way out in space. The centres of urban population were clearly picked out in red, revealing that the whole of the North American eastern seaboard (from Newfoundland to Florida) was heavily populated. I told Pat that if this was the present situation, then by 2010 it would be an urban sprawl, so why not combine the cities into one vast city."

As with many eighteen-year-old recollections, Kevin O'Neill recalls a slightly different version of this key event in Dredd's development: "When Doug Church saw Carlos's city-scape poster he said it was not just New York, but it was a mega-tropolis, and Pat Mills soon dubbed it the world's first Mega-City...hence Mega-City One."

However it was named, Ezquerra's vision of the Mega-City set the tone for Dredd's future environment, but it posed another dilemma for Mills. Wagner's projection to 2010 was now way too short to realistically fit the massive urban growth Church envisioned. So Mills was forced to change the original setting from the early part of the twenty-first century to the final year to allow for the futuristic city-scape. This time-stretch also helped solve another problem Mills had been frantically trying to accommodate in the story – Ezquerra's very futuristic-looking uniform.

Mills knew he had to improve on the censored first strip, but Ezquerra had shown visually that the character was definitely worth the time and effort. So Mills started by working out what hadn't worked effectively in the first strip. What had stood out most, in Mills's opinion, as the most incongruous element of BANK RAID was the first crime had been just that. A bank raid seemed far too conventional a crime for 2099 AD in lawless, downtown Mega-City One.

Mills was forced to find a more suitable future crime to open the files of Judge Dredd. This search was no easy feat, as the *story behind the story* took more twists and turns than a Mega-City skyway and problems loomed as large as a Mega-City star-scraper.

> "The first strip was set right in the middle of New York City, some years in the future – so I decided to make the buildings rounded and soar into the air, to house the many millions of people. This was the shape I drew the city."
>
> *CARLOS EZQUERRA – JANUARY 1995*

# TWO SIDES TO EVERY STORY

The story behind the search for the first published Judge Dredd story does indeed have two stories – official and actual. The well documented official story behind the first published Dredd strip is a simple linear progression.

THE OFFICIAL STORY

1. Since BANK RAID was considered too violent and set in the wrong period, Pat Mills found himself short of a first story.

2. Short of time before the launch of *2000 AD*, Mills wrote a second Dredd script – THE NEW YOU, which included the necessary changes (in time and look) from BANK RAID.

3. Happy with the result, Mills did not consider his story strong enough for a first episode and set about writing a third story.

4. Taking an opening idea from freelance writer Peter Harris, Mills gelled it with a closing device suggested by assistant editor Kelvin Gosnell.

5. This JUDGE WHITEY story suited Mills's requirements for the first published strip.

6. Mills was then faced with another problem. While writing THE NEW YOU and JUDGE WHITEY scripts, his first choice artist Carlos Ezquerra returned to work full-time for *Battle*. So, Mills was forced to entrust the first published Dredd strip to unpublished artist Mike McMahon.

7. Using Ezquerra's original visualisations and BANK RAID strip, McMahon was able to do a fair copy of Ezquerra's style and the rest, as they say, is history.

For the past eighteen years, this has been the *official* story that has been given to *2000 AD* readers. As shall be seen, the "actual" story is far from being such a smooth progression, which Mills readily owns up to: "It's not that the *official* story is incorrect, it's just that it is a simplification of what actually happened. As the years progressed and we looked back, we didn't think anybody would care about the *actual* story...we didn't know the story would still be going strong almost twenty years later. It wasn't a case of deliberately misleading people – it was simply an easier story to remember and relate."

In order to keep control over work-in-progress and payments, editors keep a make up ledger which details when and who wrote, drew and lettered every piece of work that goes into each issue. Needless to say, with a comic as rule-breaking as *2000 AD*, some of this detail was not fully recorded, while other bits of information have been entered – mostly in pencil – and other notes rubbed out.

After piecing together the ledger's information and editorial comment, it was obvious that the *official* story no longer fitted so snugly. Quite clearly there was no linear progression from BANK RAID to JUDGE WHITEY via THE NEW YOU.

Backed up by the faded pencil ledger entries, a convoluted series of sagas and setbacks began to emerge. Firsthand interviews with writers and artists didn't so much clarify the story in many cases as serve to increase the intrigue involving censorship, foreign affairs, contract disputes, artistic walk-outs and missing scripts. All this off-page drama was set against a fast approaching deadline for a new style comic – which had other equally demanding new stories in development.

"It's very difficult to remember, after eighteen years, with all the writing and rewriting, who actually wrote the early stories. What makes it even more difficult is that back then we hadn't won the battle and got the credit boxes on."
*KELVIN GOSNELL – FEBRUARY 1995*

[Right] *The key to discovering the "actual story behind the story" came from the* 2000 AD Make Up Book Prog 1-44.

JNP 13 UNSCHEDULED MATERIAL                                   JUDGE DREDD

| NO | ITEM | DESCRIPTION | SCRIPT | PAID | STORY / ARTIST | PAID | COMMENTS | SCHEDULED |
|----|------|-------------|--------|------|------|------|----------|-----------|
| 1 | JUDGE DREDD | STATUE OF JUDGEMENT | MALCOLM | 42.50 | SALINAS 15/10 | 40 | First two pages commissioned only | ISSUE 17 USED |
| 2 | " | " | " | | | 36 | (artist unknown quantity - unlikely to be No 2) | |
| 3 | " | " | " | | McMAHON | 144.00 | | |
| 4 | " | " | " | | | | | |
| 1 | JUDGE DREDD | BODY SNATCHERS | MALCOLM | 42.50 | MIKE McMAHON | 144.00 | DRAWING ALL PAGES ON SPEC. | 4 PAGES USED |
| 2 | " | " | " | | " | | Back - GREAT. | ISSUE 6 |
| 3 | " | " | " | | " | | ✓ | |
| 4 | " | " | " | | " | | ✓ | |
| 1 | JUDGE DREDD | COURT ROOM | CHRIS LOWDER | 32.00 | | | | (?) |
| 2 | " | " | " | | | | | |
| 3 | " | " | " | | | | | |
| | (?) | " | " | | ESQUERRA (14/10) | | | |
| 1 | JUDGE DREDD | MUGGER'S MOON | GERRY | 45.22 | COOPER | 192.50 | OK ✓ paid 18.00 + 4.50 | USED ISSUE 19 |
| 2 | " (MUST 2) | | | | " | | JACK POTTER 4/4 Scheduled for No 8 | |
| 3 | " | " | " | | " | (5@ 38.50) | | |
| 4 | " | " | " | | " | | | |
| 5 | " | " | " | | " | | | |
| 1 | JUDGE DREDD | SUICIDE | KELVIN 25/10 | 42.50 | MIKE McMAHON | 144.00 | Rec'd 30/11 Bloody good! | USED IN ISSUE 3 |
| 2 | " | " | " | | " | | | |
| 3 | " | " | " | | " | | | |
| 4 | " | " | " | | " | | | |
| FOUR PAGES | JUDGE DREDD | CAR SNATCHERS (1) | CHAS HERRING | 42.5 | BELARDINELLI 30/11/76 | 168.00 | Inv 387 4/1/77 | USED IN PROG 8 |

It was found, from the ledger and interviews, that Pat Mills had commissioned fifteen single episode Dredd scripts after BANK RAID and before the launch of *2000 AD* in February 1977. Some dates are still not known, but the chronology has been backed up by firsthand interview.

## DREDD SCRIPT CHRONOLOGY (from ledger)

| Date | Title | Writer | Artist | 2000 AD Prog |
|------|-------|--------|--------|--------------|
| 14/10/76 | Courtroom | J. Adrian | (C. Ezquerra) | – |
| 15/10/76 | Judge Whitey | P. Harris | M. McMahon | 2 |
| 15/10/76 | Statue of Judgement | M. Shaw | M. McMahon | 7 |
| 25/10/76 | The New You | P. Mills | M. McMahon | 3 |
| **/10/76 | Frankenstein 2 | M. Shaw | M. McMahon | 6 |
| **/10/76 | Mugger's Moon | G. Finley Day | J. Cooper | 19 |
| **/11/76 | Videophones | M. Shaw | M. McMahon | A |
| 15/11/76 | Wreath Murders | M. Shaw | M. McMahon | 24 |
| 25/11/76 | Brotherhood of Darkness | M. Shaw | M. McMahon | 4 |
| 30/11/76 | Antique Car Heist | C. Herring | M. Belardinelli | 8 |
| 19/01/77 | Krong | M. Shaw | C. Ezquerra | 5 |
| 24/01/77 | Mutants | M. Shaw | M. McMahon | ? |
| **/01/77 | Brainblooms | J. Wagner | M. McMahon | 18 |
| 18/02/77 | Whitey's Brother | S. Moore | M. McMahon | A |
| 21/02/77 | Robots | J. Wagner | R. Turner | 9 |

Other than Pat Mills, the writer most responsible for the early feel of Dredd was Malcolm Shaw, who wrote seven of the first fifteen scripts. Born in Paisley, Scotland,

Shaw was another who learnt his craft at D.C. Thomson. He joined IPC as a sub-editor, and later became editor of *Misty* – the girls' equivalent of *2000 AD*. In the early 1980s he went freelance but died after a battle against cancer soon afterwards. He is remembered by IPC Art Editor, Jack Cunningham: "Malcolm was widely held in regard as a writer – he was very inventive and imaginative. If he had graduated from the comics business he could have become a writer of consequence. But Malcolm loved comics and had a great enthusiasm for the business, and even though he had the chance to go into TV scriptwriting, he felt he couldn't work in both fields, so he chose to stay with comics."

How Shaw and his contemporaries fitted into this cauldron of creative coalition, is explained by Pat Mills: "As with any house character, it was normal for me to put Dredd out to every writer who came into the office. I would have given anybody a go at Dredd – Jack Adrian, Malcolm Shaw, Charles Herring and Peter Harris. It was the same principle I'd used on *Action* – farm it out and see what they all came up with. Since I didn't want to write the stories myself, I had to find someone who did and could."

According to Nick Landau (ex-acting editor of *2000 AD*), this approach was typical of Mills: "Pat had a sort of a shotgun approach and it's quite easy to think he would have fired off ten scripts to different artists. The thing to remember is that at the time nobody really knew what they wanted. Pat, who was leading the team, didn't know what he wanted. Part of the reason for this was Pat's constant refining of the scripts and the artwork – but the effect was great. Pat did an excellent job but he couldn't sit down and define what exactly he wanted."

This view is borne out by Mills: "The bottom line was I didn't like any of the first four or five stories that were sent back to me – they weren't necessarily bad or wrong, they just weren't right for what I wanted. How could they? My own damn stories weren't right. It showed how determined we were to get the definitive story right – a process that doesn't appear to happen in comics today."

Although he wasn't happy with any of the scripts he'd received back, Mills knew that he would have to use most of them to fill the pages of later issues. So, he needed to get them drawn. Even then, Mills found that his hands were tied as to who he could get to draw the Dredd strips: "John Sanders had a deal with Studio Giollitti to provide artwork from Italy and Argentina. Some artists were great, others were crap. There had been a long tradition of using foreign artists in British comics, because not only were they cheaper but they were far looser and more flexible than their British counterparts, who were notoriously stiff and old-fashioned. By the mid-1970s, many foreign artists too had become set in their ways and were coming to the end of their usefulness."

Mills also faced home-grown hostility from art agencies: "The agents would refuse to let me use their best British artist and suggest I use one of their foreign clients instead."

On *Battle*, Mills had been happy to use overseas artists, but, as Nick Landau points out: "On *2000 AD*, Pat required a greater degree of communication between editor, writer and artist – which became quite significant, because very often something would go drastically wrong in translation: "I remember one *2000 AD* strip we sent to a Spanish artist described a huge North Sea oil-rig; what came back was Aladdin's lamp in the middle of the sea."

Although he was forced to look abroad, Mills knew the ultimate solution to his artistic woes lay closer to home: "I was aware that there was a potential of home-grown s-f artists, who had the sort of imagery I'd seen on the covers of sci-fi paperback novels. I used to rip covers off and send them to artists for direct art references. I was after hip, modern, fresh imagery, but I was stuck with the dated Italians and Argentinians. I didn't know where to get hold of these new British artists, they had yet to come out of the woodwork."

To Mills, it seemed everyone with any interest in British comics and sci-fi was hoping that he would fail: "I also felt there was a British s-f fandom that refused to work with *2000 AD* because it wasn't taking science-fiction the way they wanted. To them it was violence dressed up as s-f. These people still saw s-f as being Joe 90 or Jet-Ace Logan, but not Judge Dredd." One such sci-fi expert who did not overly impress Mills was Arthur C. Clarke: "He may be a smart-ass and he knows all these things about this, that and the other, but a lot of his characters are fucking boring and wouldn't make good comic material. *2001* was a brilliant film but the characters are lousy. In a comic, you must start with good, strong characters."

Without a decent first script, Mills commissioned further scripts from Malcolm Shaw and *Action* writer Gerry Finley Day, whose memory is somewhat clouded: "I can't remember in what order the early Dredd stories were written. All I can recall is that there was madness in the office trying to get everything together for the first few issues."

Mills sent four of the first five commissioned scripts to different artists: Horacio Lalia and Alberto Salinas in Argentina, John Cooper (who'd almost got the nod over Carlos Ezquerra to draw the initial Dredd visuals) and one to a newly discovered Chelsea Art College graduate – Mike McMahon. Mills knew the scattering of scripts had been forced upon him: "I had a whole bunch of scripts with artists at the same time because I knew I would need more than one story since Dredd was going to be an on-going series. I got a whole bunch drawn and then juggled them around into whatever order fitted. This explains why the first stories were self-contained single episodes – which the reader seemed to like rather than the more usual multi-week storylines."

As well as new artists, Kevin O'Neill recalls Mills's efforts in discovering the true Dredd writer: "Pat was always trying out new writers on Dredd. People such as Gerry Finley Day and Malcolm Shaw who were on the fringe of girls' comics and Jack Adrian, but his stuff didn't work out."

Jack Adrian (aka Chris Lowder), a major contributor to *Action* with his 'Kids Rule OK' and 'Dredger' scripts, was to have an equally devastating effect on the way Judge Dredd was to develop. Although he is destined to be remembered as a writer whose total Dredd output was banned, Adrian's first Dredd script COURTROOM was to set off a series of far-reaching consequences.

# ROOM WITH A PHEW!

"I was told by Pat to write something as absolutely violent as I could. So I came up with an execution theme inside a special courtroom, where criminals were sentenced to death and then executed. I had visions of blood running down into runnels and flowing out the courtroom."

*JACK ADRIAN – JANUARY 1995*

One of the first scripts Mills commissioned in autumn 1976 was Jack Adrian's COURTROOM. Adrian explains the background to his story: "When Pat asked me to write COURTROOM he didn't give me any indication of how far into the future it was to be set. But it was definitely not the end of the 21st century. I don't think Pat had fully fleshed out Dredd's background by then.

"One thing Pat did make clear was that this story was to be the first half of a two-parter, and I had to reach a point at frame fourteen where the second half of the story would pick up with a Judge riding along a skyway past a huge crumbling skyscraper.

"It was done as a connecting piece with another script, so it should have dovetailed into something that had already been written about some thugs holed up in some derelict multi-storey.

"A reference to out-of-town hick judges was my own invention and not something Pat had planned. I just felt the way the story was going that Dredd would be the best and most efficient Judge in America.

"Also, the plot of having Dredd punish a citizen who cheers on the execution was again something I dreamt up for my own story. I hadn't seen Carlos's original [BANK RAID] strip which had a similar scenario.

"But my story was soon deemed too violent and too unpleasant for publication – I'm not sure who by, probably John Sanders, but Pat may have stopped it going any further. This was a real pity, because the story was originally slated to be used in the first five stories of the new strip."

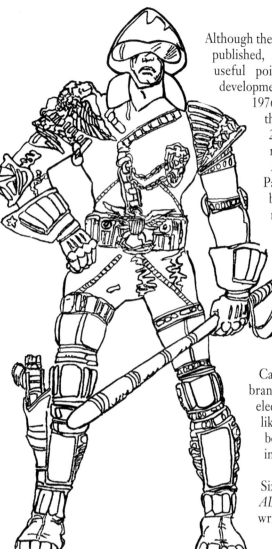

Although the script was never even drawn, let alone published, Adrian's original script does give a useful pointer to Dredd's and *2000 AD*'s development. The script is dated 13 September 1976, a month earlier than suggested in the *Make-Up Ledger*, and at that time, *2000 AD* had yet to be named – Adrian referred to it as *New SF Paper*.

As with most script ideas he sends out, Pat Mills also forwards a welter of background information; Adrian remembers his package: "The script was done before I received Carlos's original [BANK RAID] strip. All I had was a monochrome stat of Judge Dredd riding along the skyway. This was originally planned to go into a story but was finally used as a back-page poster.

"I also received this stat of Carlos Ezquerra's revised Dredd figure, brandishing this weapon, which was electrified in some bizarre way – rather like John Wagner's Electro-Knux which both Johnny Alpha and Wulf later used in the original 'Strontium Dog'."

Six months prior to the launch of *2000 AD*, and a few days after Jack Adrian had written his COURTROOM script, the

*[Left] This photocopy of Ezquerra artwork – a later variation on his initial visuals – has never been published before.*

furore surrounding *Action* came to a head, as the writer painfully remembers: "After I sent in my first script I was supposed to have done more but, a few days later, *Action* was pulled and everything fell apart." Ironically, Adrian himself had more than a hand in *Action*'s demise.

The 18 September 1976 issue of *Action* [see right] cost sevenpence, worth every penny just for Carlos Ezquerra's controversial cover of Jack Adrian's nightmare vision depicting Britain's rioting youth – with a provocative headline.

Distasteful as some may have found the cover pic, this wasn't the *straw dog* that broke the camel's back. Neither was it other incidents from Adrian's 'Kids Rule OK' strip: a kid is shot point-blank in the stomach with a shotgun, other kids make and throw petrol bombs, and two other kids shoot each other with shotguns.

Kelvin Gosnell pinpoints the offending strip:

[Below] A few days after the offending issue of Action went on sale, the Daily Mail led the national media condemnation. The newspaper included the four frames that inflamed public decency.

"What horrified many was a scene from Tom Tully's soccer story 'Look Out For Lefty', where the hero's girlfriend chucks a bottle on to the pitch and hits a player, and the hero says to himself "*Good ole Angie!*". Tully should have been shot at dawn for a year for writing that. That was the reason the comic was pulled, because the hero had praised an act of vandalism. It went all the way to the House of Commons, with John Sanders meeting Willie Whitelaw, the Home Secretary, to discuss this media backlash against violence in teen comics."

Daily Mail, Friday, September 17, 1976

# Comic strip hooligans

## Soccer chiefs hit out over bottle-throwing heroine Angie

An extract from the IPC comic Action.

A COMIC read by 180,000 children each week was accused yesterday of pandering to violence.

For one of the strips features a girl Soccer fan hurling a bottle at a player, knocking him out.

And the cover shows teenage thugs beating up a policeman, with the headline 'Aggro is a way of life in Kids Rule OK !'

The comic, Action, published for nine to 14-year-olds by IPC, was condemned yesterday as :

*Appalling and brainless* by Football League secretary Alan Hardaker, and

*Irresponsible nonsense* by Ted Croker, secretary of the Football Association.

In the strip 'Look out for Lefty,' a player tries to thwart the hero's goal-scoring attempts. But he reckons without heroine Angie and is carried off 'with blood streaming from his head' after the throws a bottle from

By JOE STEEPLES

just one child's mind, I think they're wrong.'

Even harsher words came from Mr Denis Gifford, the organiser of a comics conven-

'Just as pornography caters for a mass market for adults, stuff like this provides violence for a mass market of children. As far as the people who

may well be an excellent football administrator, has any professional knowledge of children's magazines, child psychology or what does or

Following the newspaper barrage, John Sanders tried to defend his comic on national television: "Things had come to a head when, due to the biased nature of the interview, I walked out of a live TV debate with Brian Glanville on the level of violence in boys' comics on the BBC's *Nationwide* hosted by Frank Bough. This was the sort of pressure we faced on *Action*.

"The comic was so tough and so realistic that it was actually pulled from the shelves by IPC with a very healthy circulation of around 180,000 – during my absence on holiday in Italy, where I first read the news in the *Telegraph*."

The legacy that *Action* left is encapsulated by Martin Barker, in his own detailed account – *Action: The Story of a Violent Comic*: "It was almost certain that without *Action* there would have been no *2000 AD* [and no Judge Dredd]...Writers and artists cut their teeth on *Action*, and then moved on to *2000 AD*. *Action* was the living proof that new kinds of comics could reach new kinds of readers, and create a rare kind of loyalty."

Looking back, Jack Adrian feels the sudden demise of *Action* and its subsequent relaunch in emasculated form had a direct effect on Judge Dredd: "It was interesting that if *Action* hadn't gone down the Swannee, Dredd would have been different – not vastly but he would have been developed into an alternative world.

"No explanations were given when *Action* returned...nothing. This to a certain extent influenced the direction of *2000 AD*. They figured they could get away with Dredd because he was a Judge representing law and order. He wasn't some dirty swine like *Action*'s Dredger (who may have worked for British Intelligence but still did nasty things in Britain's name), and even better, Dredd was in the future. So no one could point their finger and say that the paper was having a go at contemporary politics and current affairs.

"Even so, they didn't want things getting too nasty. My COURTROOM concept was a bit too gruesome. But, before I wrote the script, I was told quite specifically that '*there were no limits*', and that I could be as violent and gruesome as I wanted. The *Action* business did a lot of damage."

Pat Mills had his own views on why he didn't even get Adrian's script drawn: "COURTROOM may have been too violent but, the truth of it is, I didn't like Jack's version. I can't recall what it was but I just didn't like it. I recall the feel of the story wasn't how I wanted the Dredd stories to be."

Jack Adrian kindly forwarded his copy of the original COURTROOM script, which hasn't seen the light of day for almost two decades and has never been published in any form – until now...

# COURTROOM by JACK ADRIAN

**Note to Artist:** See attached sheet A for suggested lay-out for Page 1 of this story. Two-thirds of the page (down) should be taken up with a long, dramatic close shot of Dredd; something along the lines of the brilliant piece of artistic delineation roughly (mhah!) sketched out.

Sheet B contains a rough overhead diagram of the Central Punishment Court, where the action of this part of the story takes place. It's not really much like the Law Courts of today. It's a medium-sized room — fairly high ceiling. At one end is the area where the prisoners are. Running right across the room, from wall to wall, is a thick black bar. It's not held up by struts, or anything like that. Simply runs from wall to wall. This bar is where the prisoners stand. Rubber-gloved attendants make the prisoners hold the bar with one hand (they'll be in front of the bar), and then an electric current is switched on, which runs through the bar. The prisoner cannot then let go of the bar, but is "attached" to it. The current won't be too strong; they won't be jumping up and down convulsively. They are thus an ideal target for the Executioner, Dredd – who will sit at the other end of the room, in a large throne-like chair on a raised podium. He will thus be shooting slightly down at the prisoners across the other end of the room. Behind the bar, on one side of the room is a door through which the automopps will come (see in script). On each side of Dredd's "throne" are two tables. At one will sit the Clerks of the Court, the recorders, etc., while at the other table sit the medics/doctors. On each side of the room are the spectator seats – members of the press and people like that, who come to see that justice is not only done, but seen to be done. There will also be a smattering of privileged members of the public, who like seeing people getting killed. The seats are in tiers, going upwards towards ceiling – rather in manner of one of those Medical School operating rooms, where students watch surgeons performing operations. On the wall above the Electro bar is a large design of the American Eagle gripping the snake. Important to note that there should not be too many fussy details put in anywhere. The atmosphere in this Court is very clinical...cold. This is not the Law Courts, as such – this is the Punishment Court. People are not tried here – if they end up in this room, they've already been tried and found guilty. This is the room where they, ulp...get it.

## (1) Scene:
This has got to be a very Big Pic, in every sense. Dredd faces us, the reader, in a spectacularly dramatic pose. You could either have him holding his gun with his right hand, and his left hand slightly out behind him – or, probably better, so that he's holding his gun with both hands. He crouches slightly...tense and dynamic. His expression – behind his helmet-mask – is grim, hawklike – his eyes almost seem to burn. The barrel of the gun is HUGE in the frame – much, much bigger than in my sketch. It's almost like a bleeding cannon we're looking down. In fact, I think we could take it that the gun is the all-important thing in this opening frame, and Dredd is not so important. We see him, sure – but the very first thing that hits us as we glance at this page is the vast, sinister hole – the gun barrel.

   **Dredd**: PRISONERS AT THE ELECTRO-BAR – YOU HAVE BEEN FOUND GUILTY OF ROBBERY WITH VIOLENCE ON 17 COUNTS! HAVE YOU ANYTHING TO SAY BEFORE SENTENCE IS CARRIED OUT?

## (2) Scene:
This frame could be smaller than how I've sketched it on my rough lay-out. It's not so important as, say, Frame 3. Take this from slightly behind Dredd, looking across the room, and slightly down – at three men, holding the bar with one hand each. All three are tough, brutal, slightly Italianate men – and all three are clearly defiant. They glare back at us/Dredd...their faces twisted up into vicious, ratlike expressions of defiance and hatred.

   **1st Man:** NOT A THING, JUDGE DREDD.

   **2nd Man:** EXCEPT MAYBE...

   **3rd Man:** ...GO TO HELL!

   **Dredd:** NO, MY FRIENDS – HELL IS WHERE YOU ARE BOUND FOR, AFTER I'VE PASSED...

## (3) Scene:
This frame should be split up into three narrow ones – something like how I've split it up in my sketch. Frontal shots of Dredd...slightly blurred to show speed. His gun to our left in the first frame...straight at us in the next...and to our right in the 3rd. There are three connected speech balloons running along the top of the whole picture. Emphasize the lithe, tigerish speed of this dynamic, but ice-cold, killing machine.

   **Balloon 1:** ...SENTENCE...

   **Balloon 2:** ...OF...

   **Balloon 3:** ...DEATH!

**(4)Box:**
IN MANHATTAN'S CENTRAL PUNISHMENT COURT, 21ST CENTURY JUSTICE HAD JUST BEEN PERFORMED AT THE ELECTRO-BAR...BY JUDGE DREDD!

**Scene:**
A narrow shot of Dredd, full-length. He'll still be standing on his podium – but here he's facing us, holding his gun on the palms of both hands, and looking down at it, sombrely, broodingly. We don't see anyone else in this shot, either – just the tall sombre figure of Dredd.

> **Dredd:** WELL, GENTLEMEN...?

**(5)Scene:**
Angle this from Dredd's right boot – the one with the holster in it (holster's empty, of course, since Dredd's still holding his gun). The boot is large in the frame – all we see of Dredd, and we're looking past it – a sort of worm's-eye view across the court at the Prisoners' Area. Here we see three white-coated men – the medics – checking the bodies. The three men hang limply from the bar, clearly dead. The medics wear rubber gloves and boots – very clinical. One is applying a stethoscope to a body, and not looking up. Another is peering down at the eyes of one of the dead men. The remaining doc turns towards us, looking up past us. This is the 3rd doc. He has a sombre expression on his face. Maybe wears glasses.

> **Stethoscope doc:** THE RESULT WAS NEVER IN DOUBT, JUDGE DREDD...

> **3rd doc:** THE CONVICTED FELONS ARE ALL DEAD.

**(6)Box:**
AS WAS THE CUSTOM, MEMBERS OF THE PUBLIC PRIVILEGED TO WATCH EXECUTIONS, CLAPPED QUIETLY...

**Scene:**
We now get a view, of some of the members of the "audience", on one side of the room. We angle in on three men – or two men and one woman. They all have grave expressions on their faces, and are all clapping – but not wildly or enthusiastically. Their cupped hands come together lightly...quietly. There must be no sense that they have just seen something enjoyable. It's all very decorous. Of course we see other members of public above and around them – but we angle in on these three, who are talking quietly (not whispering in a secretive manner – just talking quietly amongst themselves). Commenting. The 2nd Man nods his head gravely.

> **Woman:** NEAT AND HUMANE. ONCE THEY'RE MADE TO GRASP THE ELECTRO-BAR, THE CURRENT RUNNING THROUGH IT HOLDS THEM STEADY.

> **1st Man:** EVEN SO, DREDD'S NOT LIKE SOME OF THESE OUT-OF-TOWN HICK JUDGES, WHO MISS THE TARGET. I SEEN SOME POOR SAPS WRITHIN' IN AGONY AFTERWARDS. THEY HADDA BE DONE AGAIN.

> **2nd Man:** OLE JUDGE DREDD'S A SURE-SHOT, RIGHT ENOUGH.

**(7)Scene:**
We now switch to the rear of the court, behind the Prisoners' area. We angle in on two attendants, suitably garbed. They're near the door shown on my sketch. The 1st man jerks a thumb towards the door, while the 2nd man nods. Both have serious expressions.

> **1st Man:** SWITCH OFF THE CURRENT, CASEY, AND SEND OUT THE AUTOMOPPS.

> **2nd Man:** OKAY, BUT THERE AIN'T MUCH RED STUFF. THERE NEVER IS WHEN JUDGE DREDD'S IN COURT.

**(8)Scene:**
Close on the Automopps (two of them), as they trundle around the Prisoners' area. We see that the dead bodies are being taken away towards that side-door. The Automopps must look rather funny – slightly ridiculous – but definitely futuristic. My sketches make them look like something out of World War Two! They're rather jolly little things that clean up the mess after executions....wash down the floor, mop up blood (if any)...clean up generally. Revolving nozzles spray water from somewhere on top of them. Very close on these two. But, beyond them, in background, we see Judge Dredd and another man – man is a recorder...dressed in schoolmaster-like gown – but more 21st Century. Maybe he wears one of those four-cornered caps that French Judges wear. He speaks to Dredd, but Dredd is looking at a sheet of paper he has in his hands. Important to centre attention on the weird Automopps – so that Dredd and Recorder are really in b/g.

> **Automopps:** BLEEP BLEEP SQUISH
> WHUNNKA WHUNNKA SLURRP

**Recorder:** ANOTHER JOB OVER, JUDGE DREDD...

**Dredd:** ON THE CONTRARY, MR. RECORDER. MY CHARGE-SHEET READS EIGHT MEN – I ONLY EXECUTED THREE. BY MY RECKONING THAT LEAVES FIVE STILL TO GO...

**(9) Scene:**

Now close in on Dredd and the Recorder. They are talking quite near to the front of one of the audience areas, so we maybe see a few faces in b/g. The recorder is slightly to one side, looking very worried...nervous...wincing slightly. Dredd is looking at floor, frowning, stroking his chin with his gloved hand...almost puzzled.

**Recorder:** THE REST OF THE ANDEROZZI GANG. YOU KNOW HOW IT IS, JUDGE – WE ORDERED THEM TO PRESENT THEMSELVES FOR EXECUTION, BUT...BUT...

**Dredd:** THEY WOULDN'T COME, HUH? STRANGE – I CAN'T IMAGINE WHY...

**(10) Scene:**

We now get a large close shot of one of the front members of the audience we're near. This guy is an oaf. There's one in every crowd. He's hooting with laughter...bit mouth wide open, roaring with oafish laughter. Guffawing...slapping one knee. A really unpleasant type of creep.

**Creep:** HA-HA-HA! I LIKE YA STYLE, JUDGE! MAYBE THEY SIMPLY DIDN'T WANNA DIE? HA-HA-HA!

**(11) Scene:**

Quick change of atmosphere. Close on Judge Dredd – large in the frame. With one hand he is beckoning to the man, while drawing his stick from its scabbard with the other. He looks stern and grim... and cold. The man is slowly getting off his seat, white-faced, and coming down towards Dredd – clearly quaking with fear.

**Dredd:** I WOULD REMIND YOU, CITIZEN, THAT YOU HAVEN'T JUST BEEN WATCHING A CARNIVAL SIDE-SHOW. IF YOU CANNOT RESTRAIN YOURSELF IN THE COURTS OF JUSTICE...

**(12) Scene:**

Good action shot, here. Dredd is beating the living shit out of the guy – using his stick one-handed. We maybe see three or four "sticks" as they batter down the guy – a blurred effect, to show that the stick is raising and falling. The guy is being battered to his knees, gasping and gagging with pain – he's pleading and apologising at the same time. From this angle, we can see the stern faces of some of the audience, one of whom is whispering to another.

**Dredd:** ...THEN I'M GONNA HAVE TO RESTRAIN YA MYSELF!

**Creep:** UGGH! M-MY APOLOGIES...JUDGE DREDD! AAAGH!

**Man:** THE JUDGE IS A HARD MAN. RESPECT FOR THE LAW IS REAL SACRED TO HIM.

**(13) Scene:**

Close on the Recorder. He comes quickly across the floor towards Dredd, who turns towards him. The creep is cowering on the floor. The Recorder is accompanied by a couple of ordinary cops.

**Recorder:** 'SCUSE ME BUTTIN' IN, JUDGE, BUT WE JUST HAD A FLASH THAT THE REST OF THE ANDEROZZI GANG ARE HOLED UP IN A DERELICT MULTI-STOREY DOWN TOWARDS THE BROOKLYN FLYACROSS. DO WE SEND A PATROL OUT TO BRING 'EM IN...?

**(14) Scene:**

Take this from just above ground-floor level, as Dredd comes towards us, striding purposefully towards us. He's pushing his stick back in its scabbard. He looms above us...a tall grim vengeful figure. Behind him we see the Recorder, cops, etc., looking our way, at his departing back. The creep is crawling away towards his seat. But Dredd is the main figure in this shot.

**Dredd:** THAT WON'T BE NECESSARY. I CAN DEAL WITH THAT TRASH MYSELF...

**Note [to Pat Mills]:** As far as I can see, this will now dovetail fairly easily with what remains of the story that you hold – since the next scene will be the Flyover, and the deserted Multi-storey.

This sequel story, which Adrian refers to in his final note, turned out to be JUDGE WHITEY – the first-ever published Dredd strip, so Jack Adrian came very close to writing the debut Dredd story. The reason why COURTROOM was never even drawn is obvious to anyone who reads the original script, as Adrian admits: "It was never used because it was too violent and, more importantly, too nasty." This censored strip had major repercussions as Adrian explains: "Coincidentally, Carlos Ezquerra was going to have drawn my script – it was to have been his first script after the censored BANK RAID strip he'd drawn."

The fact that Ezquerra was slated to draw Adrian's COURTROOM script was down to two factors. Firstly, Mills originally saw Adrian as the writer who might come closest to his own vision of a violent Dredd, and secondly, Ezquerra had been very happy and successful drawing Adrian's strips for *Action* – so Mills decided to stick with a winning team. This team selection backfired with Graham Taylor-like proportions, a case of "*Do I not like claret!*"

With the bloodthirsty COURTROOM script being quickly censored and withdrawn, Ezquerra was left without a script to work on. Since all the other scripts had been dispatched to other artists, this created a dilemma with the artist that would escalate Mills's problems in the next stage of Judge Dredd's gestation period.

# CARLOSS

> "Ezquerra had sent in roughs of Dredd which they liked, but his drawn strip was dumped, for various reasons beyond anyone's real control and Carlos got the hump – and didn't work on Dredd again for a long time."
>
> *RON SMITH – JANUARY 1995*

Having worked with Carlos Ezquerra on previous comics, Pat Mills knew he could be a little difficult to deal with and an early episode in Dredd's development gave a hint of things to come: "Carlos had asked for a little more money to do the Mega-City poster-pic. But I had these bloody accountants breathing down my neck all the time. I was in this hostile environment where they were trying to close me down, and everything I did, everything I commissioned was queried. I may even have got Carlos another £10 for his back page, but I know he wanted more – and I still feel guilty about it to this day."

With mounting pressure, from within IPC, threatening to close *2000 AD* before it was launched, Pat Mills needed a temperamental artist like a Judge needed a temperamental vending robot: "When I asked Carlos to come onto Dredd full-time, he wanted more money and I couldn't pay him any more. I wish in retrospect I'd been able to. I think that his agent Barry Coker was not as enthusiastic about *2000 AD* and felt that staying with *Battle* would be a better bet – financially."

The then editor of *Battle Picture Weekly*, Dave Hunt, agrees with the way Pat saw Carlos's situation: "Pat was in charge of all new comics and seconded Carlos from my *Battle Picture Weekly* to draw the preliminary Dredd sketches. Carlos was very happy working on *Battle Picture Weekly* with such characters as Major Eazy and the Rat Pack, and, to be honest, I was a bit loath to see him go. As editor responsible for the look of a comic, you had to nurture new art talent and were not very keen to see it disappear.

"Carlos was so very good at the earthy, nasty feel I required for my stories. He always got the character right, but was obviously very much in demand elsewhere – he was also drawing for *Action*. Luckily for me, he seemed quite happy working on *Battle*."

Although Mills lost his influential artist, he had no regrets: "I know Carlos feels strongly about the way he was treated. All I can say is that we all did the best we could and he knew what our status was. He'd worked for me before and knew what I wanted. So he went back to *Battle*, created a character dear to his heart – El Mestizo – and it bombed."

Rumours have abounded for the past eighteen years as to why Carlos didn't draw the first published Dredd strip; one such reason is related by an equally influential Dredd artist, Brian Bolland: "I heard that Carlos had a big disagreement over his first strip and had refused to do anymore, and so he was unable to draw the first published story. It was well known within the comic world that Carlos didn't like to share any of *his* characters

[Above] *Carlos Ezquerra and his El Mestizo character.*

with other artists. Perhaps it was this slightly selfish attitude that caused his undoing on Dredd."

With his first-choice artist giving him the brush-off, Pat Mills was also without his number one writer: "John Wagner stayed out of the picture and was surprised that Dredd could work without his involvement. I saw it as John's creation, but it needed to be brought to life properly and more importantly within the context of the vision of my new comic.

"What now seems very interesting is that at this crucial time in Dredd's development his two principle creators – Wagner (verbal) and Ezquerra (visual) – for very understandable reasons, needed protecting from themselves. They'd both come up with very strong concepts and were in danger of throwing it all away. It's not a reflection on them but on the times they lived and worked in. But both did make major errors of judgement.

"Let's face it, Carlos was silly going off to draw El Mestizo, I remember thinking at the time what a stupid sod he was being, and I thought the same about John – he was just being fucking stupid over the pirate-look, but he wouldn't listen to me. Anyhow, I was determined to go ahead with Dredd looking like that. So, I was left with this brilliant character and I had to do something with him."

Looking back after eighteen years, Carlos Ezquerra has mixed feelings over the whole episode: "I was very angry that I wasn't able to draw the first Dredd story ever published, having done so much to create the visual look of the character, the city and the other elements. I had made up the character, so why not be allowed to draw the first one? I was very angry, which was maybe a bit childish, but I returned to *Battle* and continued drawing for that comic. Despite all my anger with the way I was treated and the fact I never had my original artwork returned to me, just photo-copies, I am just glad that the character of Judge Dredd which I did so much to bring to life, has helped so many British artists to make a career and a living. This fact makes me more proud than the film, or anything connected with the character. It is something that is always with me!"

No British artist gained more from Carlos's bequest to the nation than the mercurial Mike McMahon...

# THE SINCEREST FORM OF FLATTERY

"I was forced to move on without my original artist and brought in Mike McMahon who was capable of providing a fair copy of the classic Ezquerra style, as well as providing his own creative ideas."

*PAT MILLS – JANUARY 1995*

During October 1976, Mills faced a revolt from his Argentinian artists. Horacio Lalia refused to draw the JUDGE WHITEY strip – the *official* reason given has always been that Lalia found the strip too violent. But Mills remembers this slightly differently: "Lalia wouldn't have had any moral qualms, because he drew other ultra-violent strips before and after this period. He drew 'The Running Man' in *Action*, which had people having their heads cut off and blown up."

The extent to which the Argentinian artists had been causing problems is highlighted by Kelvin Gosnell: "A lot of our artists were South Americans and the excuses we used to get from these coves were absolutely unbelievable. In the office we had an excuseometer on the wall to keep a record.

"One of them literally had a grandmother who died three times, another said he'd cut his drawing finger off, and these all went onto the excuseometer, where we graded all the excuses for believability, creativity and everything else."

The ledger shows that Lalia had drawn a number of strips for *2000 AD*, including Mills's own original Hanging Judge Dread strip, 'Planet of the Damned' and 'Death Bug'. But Lalia wasn't alone in causing Mills trouble, his compatriot Alberto Salinas drew THE STATUE OF JUDGEMENT so badly that Mills scrapped his effort and started all over again on the script.

With Carlos Ezquerra his first-choice artist back on *Battle*, traditional British SF artists not giving him the time of day and foreign artists causing him more problems than a Futsie with a grievance, Mills embarked on an art trek – to seek out new CV illustrations and to boldly go where no editor had gone before. Roy Preston [sub-editor] puts this *new generation* of artist into perspective: "The revolutionary style of *2000 AD* artwork Pat demanded left many established comic artists struggling. Pat was responsible for creating a whole new school of young, British artists – whose previous experience had been in fanzines...now they had an international canvas to experiment on."

Ezquerra's defection opened up the launch pad for a young artist to rocket to stardom. It would be no exaggeration to say that Mike McMahon, considered by many to be the definitive Dredd artist, grew up and honed his talents as an artist exclusively through his work on Judge Dredd. Whilst at Chelsea Art College, McMahon had work published in the comic fanzine *It's All Lies*, and, after graduating, had produced eight pages of pencil artwork for a proposed D.C. Thomson sci-fi comic. This rival paper never appeared alongside *2000 AD* on the newsagents' shelves, but McMahon's agent Tony Kelleher took samples of these drawings to Pat Mills. Desperately still searching for fresh, local artists, Mills was instantly impressed and so began the historic partnership between McMahon and Dredd.

McMahon remembers an early but typical Dredd assignment: "The postman delivered a huge art-tube and I pulled out a script which they wanted me to draw and art references in the form of photo-prints of Carlos's first strip [BANK RAID], which I understood wasn't to be published because it featured a street-side execution. They wanted me to produce something that looked like Carlos's original, which looked great. I had been very impressed with his work on 'Major Eazy' and 'Rat Pack', and I was amazed to see what he had done in visualising Dredd."

The *Make-Up Ledger*, so useful in uncovering many forgotten secrets, proved fruitless, if not misleading, in trying to follow the meteoric career path of this new artist. With the passage of time, it has become accepted that the first Dredd strip McMahon drew was Pat Mills's THE NEW YOU, but the author reckons otherwise: "McMahon definitely drew at least one story before THE NEW YOU. I saw that story as being the first and definitive Dredd story so I wouldn't have trusted a young, untried artist with it.

"My guess is that FRANKENSTEIN 2 was the first Dredd strip Mike ever drew. I liked his first strip – it was cool and interesting and what made it even better I'd found a guy who could draw like Carlos."

Mills's memory is fully backed up by his entry in the ledger which states "*artist drawing all pages on spec*" – the standard approach when trying out a new artist. When McMahon returned the four page strip Mills wrote two words in the ledger, "*Back – GREAT*".

Although he was very happy with his protégé, Mills was also aware that the original Dredd artist was still angry: "I was amazed by Mike's artwork, but I don't think Carlos was too impressed. In some ways, Mike introduced things that Carlos doesn't have. It came as a great shock to Carlos and he was pissed off. My attitude was that he didn't want to do it, he knew the rules of the game – what was I supposed to do?"

Mills may have been delighted with McMahon's artwork, but the perfectionist in him spoke up: "I still wasn't happy with the FRANKENSTEIN 2 story, I wanted something better. I had found myself the Dredd artist – what I needed was the Dredd script to give to him. So I sent THE NEW YOU to Mike."

When McMahon returned his NEW YOU artwork, Mills was so impressed he wrote "*Bloody Good!*" in the ledger. Despite his reaction over the artwork, Mills was again unhappy with the overall plot of THE NEW YOU: "You can only get so much out of an initial idea, and despite the good aspects of this plotline it didn't carry enough weight to be the first story. A strong story needs a strongly identifiable

*[Above] McMahon's first Dredd figure to appear in a strip [FRANKENSTEIN 2], actually appears as late as Prog 6.*

villain." This echoes the same criminal deficiency in BANK RAID.

The following day after receiving McMahon's THE NEW YOU artwork, Mills sent him a completely rewritten JUDGE WHITEY script, which Lalia had originally refused to draw.

Mike McMahon had risen swiftly to the top of Mills's artistic tree and was rewarded with the ultimate prize, the chance to draw the first published Judge Dredd strip.

Having had the luxury of a year in preparing for the launch of his new sci-fi comic, Pat Mills decided the first issue, dated 5 March 1977, would contain five stories, as John Sanders proudly announces: "*2000 AD* was launched directly off the backlash suffered by *Action*, which had been attacked by the media for being too violent and encouraging hooliganism. We knew that our readers wanted violence and more violence. So we had to find a way to get round the mounting pressure groups."

The new comic, the younger brother of the notorious *Action*, received its fair share of media notice, as Kelvin Gosnell brags: "The day after launch, we managed to get ourselves on the front page of *The Guardian* with a banner headline – *Comic with a thermo-nuclear impact.*"

[Below] The opening 2000 AD spread outlines the first five new stories.

The first issue may have had *impact*, but it didn't have Judge Dredd – as Gosnell explains: "One reason that JD never made it into Prog 1 was that we couldn't get the stuff in time. Pat was also convinced that Dredd was the best of the lot and he didn't want to shoot his load all at once."

This second reason for Dredd's absence is backed up by Kevin O'Neill: "Pat held Dredd back for the second issue – which had never been done before with a new comic launch, usually all new stories are in the first issue. He used Dredd to encourage readers to buy the second issue."

The only sight Prog 1 readers had of Judge Dredd was the next week ad [see page 9] for the first Dredd story – drawn by Mike McMahon.

# A WHITEY SHADE OF POW!!

As he has already explained, Jack Adrian designed his censored COURTROOM script to dove-tail into Harris's story: "What I didn't know was that derelict skyscraper, at the end of my story, would turn out to be the Empire State Building in JUDGE WHITEY." Also, unknown to Adrian, what he received was only the first half of Harris's original script, the rest Pat Mills had discarded with good reason: "I liked the first nine frames, the rest sucked."

With both Dredd's co-creators Wagner and Ezquerra away licking their creative wounds, Mills was left to ponder Dredd's future. Having written THE NEW YOU (drawn by McMahon), Mills felt it was not a strong enough story to stand alone as Dredd's first.

Mills found the basis for the historic first Dredd story from an old source: "Peter Harris (by day an accountant) started sending me stories in *Battle Picture Weekly*. I never used them because I never liked them, but since I was desperate for new writers, I persevered with him in the hope he would write something good. I remember one horrible story we bought off him, but never used, called 'Four Green Tank Men' – that was the fucking standard of most of the stories coming in from nearly all my writers. Peter continued to send me stories when I was doing *Action*. I naively kept him interested and he eventually came up trumps with one good idea – the Judge Killing."

Using the first nine frames of Harris's script, Mills manufactured a middle and end, and thus the first published episode was a triple amalgam:

**1.** Harris supplied the premise of the opening Judge Killing, the awesome sight of the Empire State Building dwarfed by roads and star-scrapers, and a riderless bike returning to Justice HQ. It was the far-reaching concept of the Judge System that was a major reason for Mills using Harris's idea first up: "The roots of the Judge System were sown by Peter Harris in the first episode with the death of a Judge being avenged by Dredd, who is part of a larger body. We could have kept Dredd a solitary lawman [as suggested in BANK RAID] – some would have preferred that, others like the way it has developed. I just built on what Harris had suggested."

**2.** It was at this time that Mills had chosen assistant-editor Kelvin Gosnell to be *2000 AD*'s first full-time staff editor, aware that his choice was more classically tuned into science-fiction. Gosnell proved himself worthy, supplying the idea of a Devil's Island prison from a similar traffic-prison he'd read about. The future was further delineated by having the prison surrounded by highways (literally one-mile high) jammed by an endless stream of 200 mph computer-controlled lorries.

**3.** Mills also added "some other bits that I worked out with Kelvin in the office and some thoughts of my own, primarily about the sanctity of the Judges. I had become obsessed with the idea of the Judge – his premier role, this key element and defined Dredd's persona as '*A man totally devoted to justice, who lives in a weird world, edged by humour*'."

With his first Dredd story written, Mills knew he had to get the strip drawn and quickly. Horacio Lalia had refused to draw Harris's original script, for whatever reasons, so Mills decided to stay at home and stick with his fresh new art talent, as Brian Bolland recalls: "Mike McMahon came out of obscurity in early 1977 to start his professional career with the first ever public appearance of Judge Dredd. His drawing style, at first only partially formed, was an imitation of the artist who co-created Dredd, Carlos Ezquerra. Carlos pulled out of the series early on, but here was a fresh new artist named McMahon who could do a reasonable Carlos impersonation."

"I remember Peter Harris's original script was sent to me as a reference for the early Dredd stories and it was only a page and a half – maybe just nine frames...It's strange how this short was finally turned into the very first Judge Dredd story."

*JACK ADRIAN – FEBRUARY 1995*

McMahon remembers the task at hand: "At first I thought it would be really hard to copy Carlos. I pencilled up the script, then inked it – it was supposed to be a Carlos Ezquerra impersonation, but I thought it looked nothing like it! But they seemed to like it in the office. I delivered the artwork in person to Pat Mills and his team at the huge King's Reach Tower, and they were stuck in a pokey corner – Pat, Kelvin and a couple of feet away Janet Shepherd [art editor] and Kevin O'Neill."

Pat Mills wasn't as happy as perhaps McMahon suggests with his opening JUDGE WHITEY spread: "McMahon did the first page and I hated it. I thought it was fucking awful and I still do. I made him do it again and it was even worse the second time. We didn't have time to do a third version. It was very much a last-minute decision on JUDGE WHITEY, and if there had been more time – and Mike knows this – I would have got him to redraw the first page a third time.

"When I saw his second and even worse attempt [see left], I suddenly realised I was fucked because architecture just wasn't his thing. Having discovered '*the new Ezquerra*', I suddenly discovered he didn't have Carlos's aptitude for buildings. I have the philosophy that if you stretch people they may deliver the goods. Not with McMahon and his buildings.

"Mike always used to sneer at anybody using references, he'd say '*Oh no, I'm going to get it out of my head*'. So, I could never work out why his Empire State Building looked like a crock of shit – it was so badly done. I thought he must have drawn it out of his head having refused to look at a direct reference. He later admitted that he got drunk one night and copied the building from a Jesus Blasco drawing from an old *Steel Claw* comic. Which is why it looks so ropey because it's not even taken from a proper reference."

McMahon's recollection of this is quite different: "The only time I was ever drunk was at the *2000 AD* Christmas party. I certainly never drew anything when drunk and I certainly wasn't going to jeopardise my new career, was I? Anyway, Pat sent me a Berlitz book of New York from which I copied the building. I didn't even have any *Steel Claw* stories on me then."

Mike McMahon's feelings on drawing the birds-eye view of New York may better explain Mills's misgivings: "I couldn't make head nor tale of Carlos's futuristic cityscape. Whether that was because I was young and inexperienced, I don't know. His was an organic kind of look, whereas I developed a more architectural style. I couldn't see what he was getting at, even though I really loved his Mega-City One drawing."

Despite McMahon's homage to the Spanish artist, Ezquerra was less than happy with his successor's copy-cat technique: "My large Mega-City poster had some of its detail copied in the opening story. Which again annoyed me, because nobody asked me or even let me know."

Despite misgivings from Mills and Ezquerra over McMahon's opening spread, JUDGE WHITEY's first page is everything the corresponding page of BANK RAID was not. It is dynamic, mysterious, set firmly in time and place with a sense of awe and wonder and a degree of unfolding drama. It also contains the same Ezquerra artwork that opened BANK RAID, as McMahon confirms: "The one clue Pat gave me was to leave space on the opening spread for Carlos's pic of Dredd on his bike blasting through a wall [in fact it's a plate glass window, which shows how poorly defined the BANK RAID strip had been]."

Although McMahon drew the rest of the five page strip, it was fitting that Ezquerra's lifted artwork (without the smashed window effect) set the published Dredd on its way. This literal recycling of Dredd on his bike is both typical of the way Mills used to treat artwork to secure the best results and how striking Ezquerra's original work really was.

The opening phrase "*Meet the Toughest Lawman of Them All...,*" with its mock-Hollywood B-movie sloganeering, kick-starts the strip into life with the right sort of feel and tempo for action and violence. All the elements needed to set up the opening strip and the stories to follow are succinctly stated in the opening captions. It is New York. It is 2099 AD. Small buildings like the Empire State are in ruins. There are vicious criminals and there are special lawmen called Judges. The question as to how special these lawmen were – and one lawman in particular – is about to answered.

Having been set-up by the simplicity of the opening spread, what greeted the reader on page two [see right] was...a shock! A special lawman murdered in cold-blood – these Judges were not indestructible super-heroes. The murderer was Whitey – Dredd's first adversary. This lawbreaker, unlike those in BANK RAID, had broken a law worthy of a twenty-first-century criminal – murdering a Judge. Whitey was also armed with a special weapon, a Laser Cannon, replacing the sadly outdated BANK RAID flame-thrower.

The criminals' hopes that the fallen Judge is Dredd are dashed by a close-up of the breast badge – Alvin. This minor detail marked another distinct improvement from BANK RAID, in which Dredd wore a badge with *Judge* on it. This old-style badge can just be made out on the Ezquerra artwork in the opening frame.

This individual ID idea was Mills's master-stroke: "One underlying theme of comics is to assume the reader is not particularly bright and explain and signpost everything as simply as possible. The badges are a good example. Originally Carlos carefully drew *Judge* on the breast badge, but we felt that when Judge Alvin was killed in the first episode we needed to identify each Judge (particularly since they all look similar under their helmets). But Mike only drew the names on crudely, something I now regret not making him go back and change. But at the time I was chasing a hundred and one different things and didn't have time."

Unlike Dredd's "in-yer-face" entrance in BANK RAID, his debut is dramatically delayed until after he has been seriously maligned by the gang members, who also reveal the professional respect they have for him as an

TRIVIA NOTE: The name Whitey was previously used by Mills in 'Invasion' (Prog 1 of 2000 AD) for a neighbour of Bill Savage. This became the first Dredd character name borrowed from other IPC/Mills comics, and being the first Dredd criminal, Whitey lived on in the strip - making regular return visits.

enemy. Dredd's name is actually mentioned three times (in five frames) by the criminals, before he is even seen.

When we finally see Dredd he stands in a state of deference to the Grand Judge, who pays a glowing tribute to Dredd's heroic deeds – such backstory again was sadly missing in BANK RAID. For his opening words, Dredd humbly replies *"Thanks, your Honour!"*. A downbeat debut suggesting a politely-spoken, upstanding, do-gooding lawman, who knows his place and manners. Yet another mega-stroke by Mills, who knew the full impact of turning first impressions on their head, and *fucking with the reader's minds*.

Although most readers would have been happy at the first sight of the new hero-figure, Ezquerra was most certainly not: "It seemed all my creative work was being taken away from me. A Dredd figure I had drawn for the BANK RAID story was lifted and dropped into the first published story. All this without any recognition."

*TRIVIA NOTE: Ezquerra's original Dredd figure (from BANK RAID) was lifted ... but used on the cover of Prog 18.*

What Ezquerra actually refers to is a very good copy of his own Dredd figure from the first frame, last page of BANK RAID [see page 27], from which McMahon had copied the pose and style but was careful enough to reverse, making a marked change. But it was a good enough copy to fool Ezquerra – the major difference being McMahon's Dredd looks much leaner and meaner.

It must be remembered that, unlike Ezquerra's BANK RAID, this wasn't McMahon's first Dredd strip – he'd previously drawn at least three Dredd strips, FRANKENSTEIN 2, THE NEW YOU and VIDEOPHONES, so by this strip he was an old hand at drawing Dredd.

The first few frames of page three [see left] introduce us to the plot device (and an important futuristic development) of an automatic motorbike – returning to Justice HQ. This scenario is reminiscent of a sheriff's trusty steed returning riderless to the jailhouse in Hollywood B-movie westerns.

Unlike Ezquerra, who drew Dredd on his bike three times in BANK RAID, McMahon wasn't required to draw Dredd on his bike at all. The only shot of Dredd on his bike was Ezquerra's lifted BANK RAID artwork.

Although McMahon drew in the detail of the six options on Dredd's gun they are not referred to in this strip – possibly for fear of confusing the reader with too much futuristic information. Mills, again, would have realised the importance and relished the opportunity of retaining fresh material for later stories.

Dredd's first piece of major dialogue is a milestone in character development. Having been introduced in deferential mode to his superior, Dredd not only disagrees vehemently with the Grand Judge's retaliatory "bomb the bastards" approach, but suggests his own solitaire solution. Dredd's "go-it-alone" response is also ground-breaking in that the Grand Judge seemingly has a squad of Judges to call on, but he allows Dredd his wish.

This frame gives McMahon his first chance for detail of Dredd's face, helmet and badge.

At the start of page four [see right], Dredd outwits the criminals (something he didn't do in BANK RAID) using the same device that they had returned their "prize" to Justice HQ. Dredd has turned the tables on them – this is a thinking Judge...but is he an action Judge?

The next frames answer this in full – Dredd quickly becomes a man of action, diving and rolling on the floor as his gun roars ONCE! TWICE! The second shot is a masterful McMahon central spread which opens the page up gloriously, as well as emphasising the sleek majesty of this extra-special lawman. For this spread, McMahon again uses his reversed lift technique from a similar Ezquerra BANK RAID scene (see page 26), where Dredd shoots three lawbreakers.

Having killed Whitey's two henchmen, Dredd gets physical by punching the gang-leader and symbolically knocking off the Judge's helmet. Dredd's words echo those he used in BANK RAID

when he described bribing a Judge as "an odious crime!". With a life sentence passed, Dredd loads Whitey into a Police hover-transporter. Whitey's final words come back to haunt Dredd – since, in future stories, he continually manages to bust out of prison.

The fact that Dredd sentences a lawbreaker, especially an odious Judge-killer, to life imprisonment rather than shoot him in cold-blood, gives a good indication as to how far Dredd's character had been toned down from Wagner's original jay-walking scenario. As Dredd's creator admits: "Dredd was certainly watered down – I think he had to be, certainly for the publication he was in. I don't think the harsh, murderous Dredd I originally envisaged would have fitted into the comic, so they watered him down. It didn't bother me, I would have been surprised had some of the characterisation gone through untampered."

Just as the story appears ended, the reader turned to the back page of the comic to be welcomed by a glorious half-page visual feast of colour and invention – Devil's Island.

This colour spread had John Sanders purring with delight: "Dredd could be as violent as we wanted him to be, an executioner – but he was the law. The violent stories were always lightened by humour, being full of magnificently original ideas. My favourite was the Devil's Island prison where the traffic was so congested the prisoners couldn't escape. This reflected the concerns of millions of British people, at the time, who were under siege from the mounting traffic problem in urban areas. This first story showed the way forward for all Judge Dredd stories, by taking contemporary problems and transforming them into twenty-first-century dilemmas."

Kelvin Gosnell, who contributed the future prison idea, modestly remembers "everyone was very impressed with Devil's Island – it got us a lot of extra publicity". But Gosnell's contribution to the prison wasn't limited to ideas, the bearded Devil's Island inmate who explains the meaning of life to Whitey bears a close resemblance to Gosnell.

Having set up a strong plot and excellent narrative, Mills almost lets the story down through the Grand Judge's post-sentence reaction. Having previously threatened to blow Whitey and his gang into oblivion, the Grand Judge now incongruously regrets the stern life sentence Whitey has received. He shows no regret for the two criminals Dredd killed or, more amazingly, he shows no initial remorse for Judge Alvin, who was brutally slain defending the law and the Judge System.

Dredd, on the other hand, is seen paying his last respects to a fallen colleague. The dead Judges' badges hung on the wall are a reminder that these lawmen of the future are not immortal '*Judges can bleed too!*' as Whitey announced in the opening spread.

The Grand Judge's final words "*Sometimes I think we're all going to die like Alvin*" are morose but, as with Whitey, are later borne out – he is assassinated in cold-blood on the streets of Mega-City One (in Prog 89).

Dredd's final retort amply sums up his simple philosophy that permeates stories to come and ends the first story on the right sombre, yet, philosophical note.

JUDGE WHITEY is a minor masterpiece of an opening gambit in the chequered history of Judge Dredd. The fact that it was the story that Mills took a year to finally develop demonstrates the true prowess of Mills the editor, who still backs his original concept to the hilt: "I believe that if you ran JUDGE WHITEY in *2000 AD* today, with slightly updated, colour artwork, it would stand up on its own as a good story. It has everything – the bike on automatic, the ridiculous landscape, the punitive ending, blind dedication to the law – all faithful to Wagner's concept."

# THE MAGNIFICENT SEVEN

Mills also knew the search for the first Dredd stories wasn't a solo effort: "Under the circumstances, it was a miracle and a tribute to all involved that we produced something so good – in such a hostile environment. Bizarrely, the hostility actually helped us. It was a case of "*Fuck you – we'll prove you wrong!*" It gave us a very clear vision of what we wanted, because, in the end, it's what you throw away that shapes what you actually create."

It was this depth of creative vision and the need to succeed that drove Mills to decide which episodes to use and which to throw away. For the definitive first episodes, Mills chose seven stories pulled from a creative mix of half-ideas, movie and TV inspirations, multiple rewrites and rejected artwork, and involved at least five writers and three artists.

The basic plots of the first seven episodes are given – along with relevant background detail to their development.

"The first episodes of a new strip are the most definitive. Finding the right stories to start off Dredd was not a desperate search, but more a measured professional approach."
*PAT MILLS – JANUARY 1995*

### JUDGE WHITEY (Prog 2)
*Writers:* Peter Harris, Pat Mills and Kelvin Gosnell
*Artist:* Mike McMahon
> PLOT: In New York, 2099 AD, from his hideout in the Empire State Building, Whitey shoots Judge Alvin dead. Judge Dredd is sent to apprehend Whitey, which he does, sentencing him to life on Devil's Island. For detail see Chapter 13.

### THE NEW YOU (Prog 3)
*Writer:* Pat Mills
*Artist:* Mike McMahon
> PLOT: In an attempt to avoid detection, murderer "Scarface" Joe Levine has an illegal genetic face-change. But his voice pattern gives him away and, following a 200 mph chase, Dredd arrests him and sentences him to the time-stretcher jail.

Mills came up with this story before he rewrote Peter Harris's JUDGE WHITEY, and originally had this in mind as the first Dredd: "To have an immediate sci-fi impact I introduced the voice-recognition box built into Dredd's bike and the genetic face-change facility."

This was the second Dredd strip that Mike McMahon ever drew and contains some embryonic and exciting action sequences.

The story is now set in Mega-City One (previously in New York) to take advantage of Ezquerra's poster pic, which Mills tacked on to the end of the story, as he explains: "to depict Dredd riding off after catching the lawbreaker. It probably looks as if they were two separate items, but I intended them to flow together. Dredd kills this guy and carries on with his patrol *'so those who have something to fear can fear me'*, or whatever."

As Mills states: "Scarface" was killed by Dredd, but the final frame [see left] suggests otherwise. Kelvin Gosnell confirms this suspicion: "That frame got censored! Originally the bullet went *ptyong!!* right through his fucking head! That was brilliant...all these bits coming out. But it was changed. He was supposed to be dying in the next few frames. We had to sub in different dialogue about *the time-stretcher jail* to cover the management censorship. The legacy of *Action* was still being felt, even six months after it was pulled."

## THE BROTHERHOOD OF DARKNESS (Prog 4)
*Writer*: Malcolm Shaw
*Artist*: Mike McMahon

> PLOT: Mutants, from outside Mega-City One, loot the City and kidnap hostages – among them the Mayor's son. Dredd follows the mutants to their hideout beyond City limits and rescues the hostages.

The third story introduces out-of-town mutants and a 120 foot high praying mantis from a wasteland which Dredd describes as, *a wilderness from the Atomic Wars*. This landmark aspect beyond Mega-City One sowed the seeds for THE CURSED EARTH saga.

It was this mutant story that attracted Nick Landau: "The first Dredd story I saw was this *Omega Man* [a 1971 Charlton Heston mutant movie] type story and it was this that got me excited about working for *2000 AD*."

## KRONG (Prog 5)
*Writer*: Malcolm Shaw
*Artist*: Carlos Ezquerra

> PLOT: Dredd investigates a series of connected deaths and discovers the murderer to be the curator of the Movie Special Effects Museum, who turns his (King) Krong exhibit onto Dredd, who destroys the monster which falls to its "death" crushing the curator.

KRONG marked two historic aspects of Dredd artwork:
1. The first Judge Dredd cover [see below right] – drawn by Barrie Mitchell – who had also worked for D.C. Thomson and on *Action*.
2. Having left the comic under a cloud, Carlos Ezquerra returned to draw his first published Dredd strip, but Pat Mills felt it wasn't strictly for artistic reasons: "When Carlos did KRONG, it was as much a money-booster as anything else. As with all artists, he liked to have more than one pen in the inkpot."

This story of a Robot Ape (its working title) was inspired by Dino De Laurentiis's 1976 remake of *King Kong* – a fact not missed by art assistant Kevin O'Neill, who played a double role: "Around that time, I was heavily into movie special effects and had done a *King Kong* fanzine. I guess that's where they picked up the idea for KRONG. Pat was being his usual fun-loving self using my name for the ferret-faced parasite murderer and had me crushed to death under my own creation. The Kevin O'Neill in the strip didn't look anything like me, because Carlos had never met me." [See page opposite – top]

This story gave Mills the chance to introduce Dredd's home and his landlady: "The attempt to get Maria in was not just for the humour but to subconsciously work a mother-figure into Dredd's soul. You've got a guy who wanders round like a robot, and unless you're a complete geek and a robot yourself, you're going think this guy needs a little mothering. So we brought in Maria. There were so many male images in the comic, it was an attempt to work women in. It has to be remembered when we started *2000 AD*, we weren't allowed any provocative images of women, certainly no snogging."

[Above] Due to the pressure of getting the right story and artwork, the continuity of the early Dredd strips was often screwed, chewed and, literally, barbecued - the mutants are clearly feasting on a giant locust and not the mantis as Dredd suggests.

[Right] Kelvin Gosnell confirms the extent to which provocative images of women were frowned upon: "We had to censor the dream blonde slightly. There were less clothes on her when Carlos first drew her. Carlos would never get us into trouble with violence but he would always get us into trouble with sex. He could draw very sexy women."

**FRANKENSTEIN 2** (Prog 6)
*Writer*: Malcolm Shaw
*Artist*: Mike McMahon
PLOT: Dredd investigates a series of bodysnatches from Mega-City ambulances and tracks down an illegal transplant surgery run by Frankenstein 2 – whom Dredd "arrests" along with a transplant patient.

Early on, Pat Mills saw a greater significance in this story: "I seriously considered Bodysnatchers [its working title] as a first three story. It was not a bad one but I later thought it too trivial, because it didn't have enough in it to be a truly definitive first story."

This first frame of Dredd [see left] arresting Frankenstein has obviously been censored. When McMahon drew the strip, Dredd would still have been seen as an executioner being depicted shooting the lawbreaker in cold blood.

The next (censored) caption reveals he was merely handcuffed. Dredd's final words are typical of the dark humour in the strip.

This strip is historically important as the first Dredd strip drawn by Mike McMahon and the first Dredd house ad [see page 9] was also taken from this debut strip.

### THE STATUE OF JUDGEMENT (Prog 7)
*Writer*: Malcolm Shaw
*Artist*: Mike McMahon

>PLOT: Dredd quells a disturbance in the shadow of the Statue of Judgement. A gunman flees but cannot escape the wrath of Dredd, who blows him out of the sky.

Pat Mills reflects on Malcolm Shaw's early script: "It wasn't appropriate as a first story because it's quite clearly a later developed story with this massive statue." [See right]

Art assistant Kevin O'Neill recalls an early brush with the law: "The first script I read was THE STATUE OF JUDGEMENT, before Carlos had accelerated the time, and it read like a pulp magazine story. From it I envisaged Dredd to be a character like US motorcycle cop Zip Nolan (from *Lion*, see left).

O'Neill continues: "The story had been set some time before Carlos had drawn the gigantic buildings, which had not been in the stories he had been working on." This explains why the Mega-City sky-line, in this opening frame, looks as if it has been added at a later date.

### ANTIQUE CAR HEIST (Prog 8)
*Writer*: Charles Herring
*Artist*: Massimo Belardinelli

>PLOT: Dredd tracks down a gang of antique car thieves, kills three gang-members and arrests the leader Krilz.

This was the only Dredd strip ever written by Chas Herring or drawn by Massimo Belardinelli – and would have been commissioned by Pat Mills when he was still firing scripts and strips off at any one who owned a pen and was still breathing.

Herring was an IPC scriptwriter on *Battle Picture Weekly* and Belardinelli – from the Studio Giollitti stable – drew the first Dan Dare strips in *2000 AD*. The Italian artist's claim to fame on Dredd is that he caused a panic in the office when he drew in Dredd's face [see left]: "I'm not sure if I actually drew in a face, but I don't think Dredd's face has ever been drawn – by me or anyone." [See Box Feature on page 74]

Kelvin Gosnell explains the hideous face "was a blind alley that we were stuck with. Neither Pat nor I were ever happy about it, as I remember, we didn't know whether it was a good idea or not, and in the end we didn't follow it up. We censored it out."

*[Right] Gosnell also had a major interest in the stolen Morris Minor: "The very first car I bought was a rusty Morris which, if Belardinelli wasn't such a fucking \*\*\*\*, he would have drawn it properly. Since they don't have Morris Minors in Italy, it was totally wrong. 55 CCR was the registration of my first car, which we put in just for a laugh. Anyhow, my car fell apart shortly afterwards."*

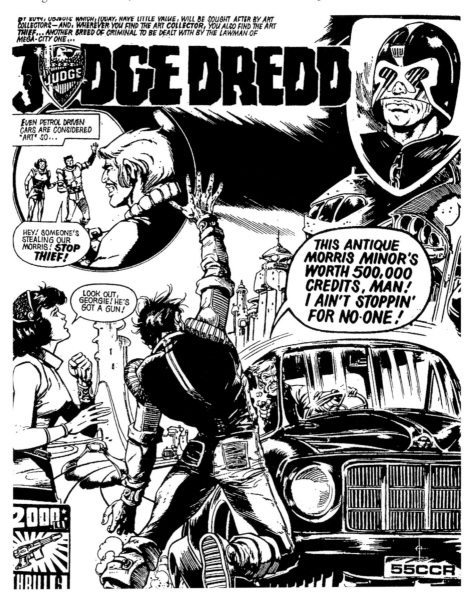

# MILLS AND BOOM!

**"Like all great editors, Pat wasn't satisfied with keeping to the norm and churning out standard work. He really wanted to make *2000 AD* different and powerful, in which the action had earth-shattering impact – a power which he used to call the Big Deal."**

*DOUG CHURCH – JANUARY 1995*

Thanks to Mills's Herculean efforts *2000 AD* was an instant success with the readers, as Kelvin Gosnell relates: "We knew we had a hit when the circulation started to go up after the end of the three-week advertising campaign on TV."

Although the comic itself was a hit, according to Kevin O'Neill, Judge Dredd wasn't a sure-fire winner: "In the first issues of *2000 AD*, Dredd was not the most popular character. M.A.C.H.1 was. He was a very conservative character, which Pat had deliberately and cleverly included to wean the readers onto Dredd and the other future strips."

M.A.C.H.1 may have broken through *2000 AD*'s sound barrier, but Mills wasn't celebrating this booming success: "I didn't feel particularly comfortable with the fact that this was the most popular character to begin with, but that's the truth. When stories like M.A.C.H.1 are written badly – they stink. But if Judge Dredd is written badly, he can get away with it because he still looks cool, the world still looks cool. It never worked with M.A.C.H.1, because he was just a guy in a suit – he just never looked or sounded good – that was his problem."

Mills gives the credit for the upswing in Dredd's popularity to one man: "It was almost a sigh of relief, for all of us, when John Wagner wrote ROBOTS [Prog 9]. That was the first story that took off, since Dredd was not the number one story in the comic until then. That is far more important than people realise since *2000 AD was* a great initial success – not due to Dredd but on the basis of every story in the comic.

"It was at the same time John returned that Dredd became phenomenally popular and I think it was at this point the other *2000 AD* stories lost their pre-eminence. I still maintain this was not only a reflection of John's ability and the strength of Dredd's character, but also the fact that the other stories had the same potential but they weren't being written by as good writers or being drawn by as good artists."

As Gosnell explains: "Pat put so much effort into all the stories, making sure they were all good. That's the way Pat was. For instance, Malcolm Shaw would write an original script, Pat and I would then discuss it at great length and decide what the best thing to do was. He'd then give the script to me to rewrite, I'd do the rewrite, give it back to him and he wouldn't like what I had done, so he'd rewrite it again. Then working together we'd do a further version. Several early stories got literally taken apart and put back together again."

Mills knew that he couldn't keep up this total rewrite to improve the script quality: "By Prog 11, it was getting more and more difficult for me to disguise this fact by papering over the cracks."

According to Nick Landau, Mills did more than paper over a few cracks: "Pat's method of writing would be to throw an idea at a writer, who would go away and write it. Pat would then rewrite it all, send it off to the artist, Pat would look at the artwork and cut it to bits and rewrite it all again to fit. Which meant the writer was treated as a human typewriter, which explains why many of them in the early days didn't feel that what they wrote necessarily ended up on the page. It was really that Pat wrote nearly every story although other writers got paid for them. But that was Pat's way. He was excellent – an extremely talented editor. It might not have been the best way of doing it but it produced the required results and it was his style. But editorially speaking, once a script came in he knew how to sub the script like no one I've ever seen. I don't think there are any editors in comics today who can edit the way Pat does."

NOT SO MUCH A SECRET AGENT MORE A SECRET WEAPON!

M.A.C.H.1

2000

THRILL 4

SUBJECT: SECRET AGENT JOHN PROBE.

PROCESS: COMPU-PUNCTURE HYPERPOWER.

DATA: COMPU-PUNCTURE IS A COMPUTERISED FORM OF ACUPUNCTURE. BY INSERTING SPECIAL ELECTRO-NEEDLES INTO PROBE'S BODY, HIS ENERGY FLOW WILL INCREASE UNTIL HE HAS THE STRENGTH OF FIFTY MEN!

* MAN ACTIVATED BY COMPU-PUNCTURE HYPERPOWER

# WAGNER'S RING OF BWIGHT WALTER

**ROBOTS** (Prog 9)
*Writer*: John Wagner
*Artist*: Ron Turner
 *PLOT*: The precursor to the eight-part ROBOT WARS saga. A blackmailer kills a number of citizens at the Robot of the Year show. Dredd tracks him down and terminates him.

**ROBOT WARS** (Progs 10-17)
*Writer*: John Wagner
*Artists*: Carlos Ezquerra (Prog 10), Ron Turner (11, 13, 16), Mike McMahon (12, 15) and Ian Gibson (14, 17)
 *PLOT*: A massive carpenter robot Call-Me-Kenneth runs amok in Mega-City One and Dredd manages to de-activate it. Dredd then resigns after his warning – that sophisticated robots will take over the city – goes unheeded. When the robots, led by a resurrected Call-Me-Kenneth, prove Dredd right he returns to action. Following a lengthy and bloody civil war against the massed ranks of robots, Dredd regains control of Mega-City One.

These robot episodes saw the return of John Wagner to the comic: "Dredd was my idea. I did the first script – which was never printed – and then didn't write another until the first of the robot stories." Pat Mills, however, remembers these Dredd stories weren't the first Wagner had penned: "John wrote BRAINBLOOMS [Prog 18] before his robot saga, but it was ROBOT WARS that really brought him back in on Dredd. John finally realised a few things – the way Dredd looked was all right, he'd created a good character in a good story, and – above all else – he should be writing it."

Mills recounts that Wagner had thrown off the mental baggage that had marred his earliest work: "John's first-ever Dredd script was political in a way that didn't make sense, it didn't mean anything, it was emotionless. ROBOT WARS was so heart-felt, it tugs at the heart-strings. You've got these poor bastards who are being melted in a cruel society, it's a reflection of apartheid, kids with no home, etc."

Wagner's most obvious socio-political comment was substituting robots for the ethnic minorities in performing menial tasks [see left], with the final scenes of freedom cruelly depicting slave-labour. The Robot stories introduced Walter the

Wobot, Dredd's faithful servant – [see Box Feature on page 63]

As Mills suggests, ROBOT WARS was literally that: "It was a robot revolution, in more ways than one – writing and artistically. You've got to bear in mind that, before Call-Me-Kenneth, there was only Robot Archie." [See right]

As with KRONG, Kevin O'Neill was to heavily influence this Dredd series: "I'd been working on a fanzine called *Mek Memoirs* written by Jack Adrian, and I complained in the office that there were no robots in *2000 AD*. I faced a tidal wave of abuse from Kelvin and Pat, who didn't want any antique robots – like Robot Archie. At the same time, John came into the office saying we should use more futuristic elements in Dredd, and so he wrote ROBOT WARS.

"Since it was a random choice as to which freelance artist would be used, I designed new characters in the office – these included Walter, Call-Me-Kenneth and the Heavy Metal Kids."

Mills was the first to admit his initial anti-robot reaction had been wrong: "Kev O'Neill was the unsung hero of the ROBOT WARS, nobody had ever come up with such unique robot designs in comics before – even in America. They really were very talented and clever designs."

Another who was impressed with the robots was John Sanders: "In Dredd, we could get away with extremely violent acts that had been banned in *Action*, because the lawman was on our side. The beheading of the big robot [Call-Me-Kenneth] was a glorious example [see below] – bits flying everywhere. It was wonderful to be able to hit back at our critics and they couldn't say anything – we had the law on our side."

Having sweated for months over the first few Dredd stories, Pat Mills realised the true Dredd story had taken shape: "It was a gripping, minor classic when compared with later sagas, but it was the first really strong epic. Until then all Dredd stories were self-contained and very few were cliffhangers. In ROBOT WARS, John managed to combine the best of both worlds – each week's story was self-contained but the whole saga was truly episodic.

"Having created the character, and then stayed on the outside for the first few months, John was able to write from the heart. Something sadly missing from the early Dredd stories."

Wagner also realised that the early Dredd stories had lacked a key element: "The point where Dredd took off was my ROBOT WARS, possibly because the quality of villains in the stories till then hadn't been very good. The readers were taken with the robots."

Mills knew that as well as the improvement in writing, his central strip also needed the best artwork to make it a complete success: "The eight episodes were drawn by a motley crew of artists – McMahon and Gibson are the only two I remember with affection. I thought Ron Turner's version was awful – despite which the story worked, which is a good example of how a magical script can survive some lousy artwork – it was a real artistic hotchpotch."

*TRIVIA NOTE: McMahon actually added an extra left arm to Ron Turner's original Heavy Metal Kids, which Turner later copied.*

One artist particularly impressed Mills: "When McMahon did the Heavy Metal Kids [see above], for the first time on Dredd we were getting really key design work. Really good stuff."

One of the most respected sci-fi artists of the 1950s, Ron Turner recalls his debut on the s-f figure of the 1970s: "The fact that my style wasn't exactly conducive with Mike McMahon's or the other artists probably explains why my contribution to Judge Dredd didn't last very long." Turner only drew one more Dredd strip – THE SOLAR SNIPER (Prog 21).

Another artist who made his Dredd debut on ROBOT WARS was the much younger and less reverent Ian Gibson (who'd drawn the 'Deathwish' strip on Wagner's *Valiant*): "I was against Ron Turner's Dredd. It was old-fashioned like a character straight out of *Roy of the Rovers*." [See right]

Despite drawing the front cover for Prog 10 [see below], the fourth ROBOT WARS artist Carlos Ezquerra was unsure of his contribution to the series: "I don't remember doing any of the early Dredd stories after my first two strips [BANK RAID and KRONG]. But at that time, I was very busy drawing all sorts of characters – I was so busy meeting deadlines I felt like the fastest pen in the west!"

This is the last Dredd strip that Ezquerra would draw for almost five years (until Prog 245). In the interim, he returned to *Battle*, and then went on to create *Starlord*'s 'Strontium Dog' with John Wagner. Kelvin Gosnell puts into perspective the original creative forces behind Dredd: "It was Carlos's character – he had designed it, but I tend to think of it as John's character from the story point of view. John developed the dark-edged humour that JD always had and really that comes in from ROBOTS."

Although, as his absence suggested, Ezquerra may have still been unhappy with Dredd, the readers were beginning to be won over, as this letter may (or may not) suggest...

*Dear Tharg,*
*It has been brought to our notice that you have been publishing a story in 2000 AD about the 21st century hero, Judge Dredd.*
*So far in your stories you have kept far enough away from the truth to keep you on the right side of the law, but* ROBOT WARS *came very close to contravening the Inter-Galactic Official Secrets Code.*
*Should you violate this Code, you will be summoned before the assembled Hall of Justice to answer charges.*
*Judge Saville*

This reader reaction marks a vitally important turning point in the acceptance of Judge Dredd as a story and as a character. After the initial single story episodes, Wagner's triumphant return meant that Dredd's development had gone full circle, as Mills roundly points out: "You have John's creation stage, my second stage to publication, John coming back in to build on that, and refining it all with an elegant humour of his own – as evidenced in ROBOT WARS."

The return of Wagner (who would continue to write the strip for the next eighteen years) saw the departure of Mills, who felt he had fulfilled his creative commitment to the comic. Just as Wagner would go on to indelibly imprint his persona on Dredd, Mills decided he had already left his mark. But Mills would himself return with two stories that became even more seminal than ROBOT WARS.

The returning Wagner fully realises the effect the departing Pat Mills had on his character: "A lot of people in the office made contributions to Dredd and his

environment, Pat Mills added a lot to the concept of it, such as Mega-City One. When I'd done it originally, I'd just set it in New York. I suppose part of it was because I was born there and grew up in the USA. It always seems to be a more natural place for the outlandish things that happen – it fits in better there than it does in this country. America's just right – there are so many oddball ideas coming out of it."

Wagner's highly influential robot saga also produced another major landmark in Dredd's career. Prog 11 marked the first issue in which the strip was moved from the ignominy of the back pages into the heart and guts of the comic. Judge Dredd had finally arrived...and the rest, as they say, is his story.

## WALTER THE WOBOT

*"Walter gave Dredd a more human dimension, in that he tolerated an annoying robot, whereas over the years Dredd became an automaton of law – dispensing justice."*
Kevin O'Neill – January 1995

ROBOT WARS **introduced many innovative robot designs, none more popular than Walter. His debut was almost his last, in a piece of Carlos Ezquerra artwork [Prog 9], as Ian Gibson recalls: "Walter first appeared almost anonymously in the background, serving synthi-caf [see below]. Wagner picked up on this and built the Walter-Maria domestic thing."**

**Pat Mills recalls a more love-hate relationship: "Wagner later developed Walter's lisp and Kevin did the brilliant visuals that took the robot idea away from Archie and made him one of the first non-humanoid robots drawn.**

**"Walter was a very important aspect of the story as he was his own creature with all sorts of components like a TV set and aerial. Having a ridiculous character who was such a useless wimp, he was very open to abuse. He was so nauseating at times – I had a healthy affectionate disregard for him."**

**Ian Gibson drew Walter many years after his first appearance: "Drawing Walter was lots of fun, when I drew** ROOKIE **[see above] for** *The Megazine* **[Progs 50-52], it was wonderful to go back to Walter and Call-Me-Kenneth again."**
**This later story, from April 1994, also illustrates one dimension of Dredd's future -** *The Megazine,* **first published in 1990, re-used a number of stories and themes from the early days.** ROOKIE **by John Wagner was a combination of his** ROBOT WARS **and** THE ACADEMY OF LAW **(Progs 34-35).**

# THREE OF A KIND

In deciding on the first seven definitive episodes and the Robot saga, Pat Mills would have discounted using at least twelve other commissioned scripts – for various reasons – to launch the Dredd strip. Some of these early scripts were never published or have simply disappeared, some were used in Annuals and others were published later in the Dredd series – BANK RAID (Annual), COURTROOM (Undrawn), WHITEY'S BROTHER (Annual), VIDEOPHONES (Annual), MUTANTS (No trace) – plus seven strips that ran consecutively (after ROBOT WARS) in Progs 18-24: BRAINBLOOMS, MUGGER'S MOON, THE COMIC PUSHER, SOLAR SNIPER, MR BUZZ, SMOKER'S CRIMES and WREATH MURDERS.

Of these, some have already been discussed in the story so far, but three need further comment, since they form part of the early Dredd evolution.

## VIDEOPHONES (*2000 AD ANNUAL 1978*)
*Writer*: Malcolm Shaw
*Artist*: Mike McMahon

> PLOT: Judge Steele goes mad and kills a number of fellow Judges, until Dredd kills him. Dredd finds out that Steele was hypnotised by his videophone, tracks the culprit down and kills him.

Some detail in this very early Dredd strip bears comparison with the first ten episodes published in the comic:

**1**. The opening page shows about a dozen Judges in sitting at a (symbolic) round table under the gaze of the Chief Judge, who has "*Called this meeting of all the Mega-City Judges*". All the judges! A mere dozen...? This shows how poorly formed the Judge System concept had been early on. Later estimates put the number of Mega-City Judges at over 50,000.

**2**. In VIDEOPHONES, Dredd has very similar dialogue [see right] to that seen in KRONG [see below] – both written by Malcolm Shaw.

**3**.The violent action shows exit wounds, something forbidden by IPC management – which may have prompted its exclusion from the comic.

**4**.The strip gives Dredd's address as Apartment 43021 in Complex Omega – in later stories, he is seen living in Rowdy Yates Block.

**5**. Judge Steele's name is seen again on the Fallen in Action plaque in ACADEMY OF LAW, despite the fact he was shot by Dredd after killing his own colleagues.

**6**. Dredd is seen riding on the left hand side of the road...normally an executionable offence. The error was down to the artist, Mike McMahon, who readily admits this was not one of his finest works: "At first I just extrapolated from what Carlos had done, reproduced his style, but after the first two stories I got cocky and my third one was rejected. When Pat first saw the artwork, he said '*If I saw that in a comic I wouldn't want to read it!*' It was bad, it ended up in the first *2000 AD Annual*!"

It was at this time that McMahon's position on Dredd was being called into question, as he relates: "I learned that some people in authority at IPC, I don't know who they were, didn't want me to stay working on the strip. If I'd known that at the time it would have crushed me, but I found out later that Pat Mills had had to fight to keep me on."

> "We always used to chat about the storylines with Pat, we were in it more for the creative buzz and the fun of it rather than the money. We were all on the same wavelength and had the same tastes."
> *GERRY FINLEY DAY – FEBRUARY 1995*

**WHITEY'S BROTHER** (*2000 AD ANNUAL 1978*)
*Writer*: Steve Moore
*Artist*: Mike McMahon
      PLOT: Whitey's boffin brother Welch holds Mega-City One to ransom, forcing Dredd to release Whitey from Devil's Island, but Dredd manages to kill Welch and return Whitey to prison.

Steve Moore is credited with writing just one Dredd strip, but his memory is not all that clear or all that happy: "I can't remember writing any Dredd story, but if my name appears on it then I suppose I may have done one. But don't ask me what it was about.

    "The little I can remember about my time with *2000 AD* is that it paid better than other comics. But to be quite honest, it was the sort of magazine that I would only write for as the last resort. I didn't like their editorial policy. My scripts were totally rewritten but still put out with my name on it, without me being consulted on either point.

    "I was also very disappointed that they turned Dredd into a super-hero. Although he didn't have any super-powers, he was very much the costumed hero. I never liked the idea of using science-fiction to continually push a central character. My idea of good science-fiction writing was always based around ideas, and as such much preferred writing 'Future Shock' stories for *2000 AD*."

Like VIDEOPHONES, this initially rejected story also has links to the early published strips:
**1.** The return of Whitey (from Prog 2) now given the full name of William Logan – another possible link to the inspirational film *Logan's Run*. Logan was also the name of a character in the early *2000 AD* Dan Dare strip.
**2.** Whitey's brother destroys the World Trade Center [see above] – which may explain why this famous landmark is never seen in any future Dredd stories.
    Again, this McMahon artwork shows his lack of architectural detail, which annoyed Pat Mills so much in the original Whitey story.

**MUGGER'S MOON** (Prog 19)
*Writer*: Gerry Finley Day
*Artist*: John Cooper
      PLOT: With a full moon in Mega-City One, Dredd kills three muggers and saves an innocent bystander. Dredd also terminates a car for polluting the purified Mega-City atmosphere.

This story was held back by Pat Mills for over four months after *2000 AD*'s launch, but according to John Cooper it was to have been used much earlier: "I should have done the first Dredd story, but MUGGER'S MOON was deemed much too violent at the time (it was the era of Mary Whitehouse), so it was postponed until Prog 19."

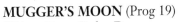

[Left] The pic that probably told against the MUGGER'S MOON strip being used early on was of Dredd's heat-seeking bullet passing through two muggers (a factor that was censored out of the BANK RAID reprint in the 1981 Annual).

Revealing the strip's age, more accurately than Carbon 14 dating, is the fact that Dredd wears a badge with *Judge* on it – predating every other published strip.

Writer Gerry Finley Day was typical of those that Pat Mills first sought out to work on Dredd, as fellow scribe Jack Adrian confides: "Gerry was a product of the public school system and was a terrific story-teller, but an abysmal scripter – the most illiterate I have ever seen. He never used full-stops or commas. You could barely work out what he wanted. He gave artists total nightmares. I recall in one script he had something like 5,000 aliens on the left, another 3,000 aliens on the right and behind them – even more.

"Once you had sorted his script out, which could take all day, you were nearly always left with a series of wonderful ideas. It was just a case of picking the gold out from all the dross."

Kelvin Gosnell recalls one such Finley Day script for *2000 AD* that was to have a lasting effect on Judge Dredd: "The word *scrotnig* comes into JD doesn't it? Pat Mills and I always had to go through Gerry's fiddly-diddly scripts enormously rewriting them, just to make out what he was saying. Have you seen one of his scripts? They're sort of like dog-sick all over a page! He couldn't type and it was difficult to find out what he meant.

"One day we came across this scene description from 'Invasion' – *Savage and men scrotnig captives across plain*. Pat and I thought what the fuck is scrotnig! It took a few minutes to work out that it was a literal for *escorting*. It was such a cool word that we felt we really ought to do something with it. So we brought it into JD as a piece of descriptive admiration – *Gee Judge we think you're really scrotnig!*

"And it's actually been photographed as a piece of graffiti on the Berlin wall. So I hope one day to see an entry in the Oxford English Dictionary that says *Scrotnig* adj. *A term meaning generally good approbation...from a typing error from Gerry Finley Day – 2000 AD 1977.*"

# SEVEN WONDERS OF THE FUTURE WORLD

**"Jack LeGrand said to me, 'This character Dredd...I don't see how it's going to work. We never see his face.' I didn't even bother to tell him that was the whole fucking point."**

*PAT MILLS – FEBRUARY 1995*

Pat Mills was constantly at odds with the IPC hierarchy: "The older management tried daily to sabotage our work with a conscious effort on censorship." These early battles with the bosses, are also relived by Kevin O'Neill: "Pat fought a war of attrition with the management, who wouldn't leave us alone. They kept reminding us that the readers were aged ten to eleven, and we shouldn't keep writing for an older audience. But the readers told us quite different – they were aged from ten to eighty. In the end, Pat became worn out and finally left altogether."

This constant management pressure was such that drastic measures were needed to keep the comic alive, as Roy Preston adds: "After thirty or so Progs, *2000 AD* was in danger of being cancelled by management who felt we were getting too far out of hand. Since we were getting so much hassle and aggravation from above, Kelvin Gosnell [who had replaced Mills as editor] felt it might be better to drop the mag, but Nick Landau refused to let *2000 AD* die.

"Back then, Dredd was far from the most liked strip in the comic, and it looked likely that it was a goner. But Nick managed to keep Dredd going, he even rigged the readers' poll by entering over fifty bogus votes for Dredd himself – to improve its popularity."

A typical reader's letter summed up the way Dredd and Dan Dare were received in these early episodes...

*Dear Tharg,*
*What has happened to the REAL space heroes who would lead and fight in rebellion, and resist against tyranny; they were noble and majestic, yet still human and understandable? Where have they gone, and what do you give us?*
*Judge Dredd is a trigger-happy man – if he is human at all – who seems to take a delight in bloodshed, as he hands out his own harsh judgements. Dan Dare is no longer the character from the old Eagle days...where once his hand was held out in friendship and peace now it holds out a weapon!*
*Adrian Gregory, Flaxton, Yorks.*

*The back cover of Prog 18 unveiled the first 2000 AD merchandise, which David Bishop [current editor of Judge Dredd:The Megazine] puts into perspective: "It always cracks me up, those early T-Shirt ads - every single character in the comic had their own shirt except Dredd. It shows you how little faith they had in the character at the start."*

Nick Landau recalls his view of the Judge's early persona: "When I joined *2000 AD*, Dredd wasn't the same character as it is now. The strip didn't sound as grand then as it does now. I thought it was a strip with a hell of a lot of potential that had been very badly written. The actual standard of writing that really annoyed me was the lack of continuity and the lack of character development, of which the same couldn't have been said of the other strips. But it was just this germ of something that looked like it could go somewhere that was really exciting."

Roy Preston puts Landau's vision into context: "Even then, Nick didn't realise how far Dredd would go, but he did know it was something worth fighting for. He also knew here was a character that could be pushed beyond the limits of acceptability. Nick would spend hours with writers and artists making sure that the strip would look and read its best. This had been something Nick had learned off Pat Mills and maybe he felt he was continuing Pat's legacy, since he had left the mag to concentrate on other projects."

DREDD

In order to launch another IPC sci-fi comic *Starlord*, Kelvin Gosnell left the daily running of *2000 AD* to Landau, Preston and O'Neill. Pat Mills fondly recalls this triumvirate: "When they took over, they really built on what we had sown in the earliest episodes. By Prog 50 [February 1978], Brian Bolland was drawing Dredd and my own CURSED EARTH saga was on the horizon."

Between Wagner's ROBOT WARS and Mills's CURSED EARTH sagas, the two writers clearly defined Dredd's psychological make-up and personal background – which projected the strip onto a higher level of creative consciousness. The following seven stories reveal how the two former writing partners, independently of each other, achieved this mega-morphosis, which set the strip up for the decades ahead.

### BRAINBLOOMS (Prog 18)
*Writer:* John Wagner
*Artist:* Mike McMahon

> PLOT: Dredd tracks down and closes an illegal brainbloom (botanical singing human skulls) farm.

The basic plot may not sound too inspiring for a key story, but it marked the return of John Wagner as writer (he wrote this story before the definitive ROBOTS WARS) and the coming of age of artist Mike McMahon [see below left].

Brian Bolland best sums up the three-way existence between writer, artist and character: "Take a good look at Dredd. Some say he's a very straightforward character, but with his face looking like a slab of raw meat, and those feet, he's a very complex and contradictory character. He's heroic and macho, he sneers and postures, but the joke is on him because he doesn't know that he looks ridiculous. In fact the joke is on some readers too, because they fail to see the fine balancing act between straight

adventure and the comic satire that's always present in a Dredd story, and at its best under the team of Wagner and McMahon."

This was Wagner's first Dredd story since the proposed management buy-out: "At the time of the failed buy-out, I was a single man and could afford to live on next to nothing. After six months away from it, I was driven back to write strips because I found I needed the cash."

McMahon explains his development as a Dredd artist: "From THE STATUE OF JUDGEMENT I stopped trying to emulate Carlos and started doing my own stuff. They liked what I was doing and said that's what they wanted from now on. I think I really got into my stride on BRAINBLOOMS."

McMahon's own view of his artistic maturity is backed up by Nick Landau: "Mick was developing faster than any other artist. It was very exciting to see how his style changed. He was extremely strong on the story-telling aspect, something not many artists have got to grips with. The essence to a good McMahon strip is his ability to portray the development of the story without dialogue. You could look at a page and immediately see what was going on, plus he'd use all these exciting camera angles."

*The first major Dredd cover on* 2000 AD *[Prog 18] was yet another 'rip-off' that angered Carlos Ezquerra. Old hand Don Lawrence drew the cover, but could not get the Dredd figure right. So Ezquerra's figure from* BANK RAID *was cut out and dropped into Lawrence's Brainbloom farm.*

## THE ACADEMY OF LAW (Progs 27-28)

*Writer:* John Wagner

*Artists:* Mike McMahon and Ian Gibson

PLOT: Dredd supervises the on-street training of rookie Judge Giant, who despite a number of mistakes becomes only the second rookie Dredd has ever passed.

This story introduces a wealth of information about Dredd and the Judge System, and the names used [see left] are very familiar. Dredd graduated in 2079 along with Judges Hunt, Wagner and Gibson – named after Dave Hunt (editor of merged *Battle/Action*), writer and co-artist respectively. The Lost in Action plaque reveals four more interesting Judge names: Mills (who somehow turns up alive and well in Mega-City 2 – Prog 85), Moore (Alan – with whom Gibson would create Halo Jones), Steele (the Judge killed by Dredd in VIDEOPHONES) and Alvin (the first Judge seen killed in action – Prog 2).

[Below] Further backstory to the Judge System was introduced in DREAM PALACE [Prog 26].

Rookie Judge Giant [see above] is a further link to another *2000 AD* story 'Harlem Heroes'.

Wagner's crèche-course concept of five-year-old cadets undergoing training [see left], eventually graduating at twenty, led to the definitive single story in Judge Dredd's history...

**THE RETURN OF RICO** (Prog 30)

*"A choice piece of Pat Mills's writing inspired some very tasty Mike McMahon artwork and to this day a lump comes into the throat of those of us old enough to remember it."*
Brian Bolland – December 1982
*Writer:* Pat Mills
*Artist:* Mike McMahon

> PLOT: Dredd's cloned twin Rico returns from twenty years imprisonment on Titan and swears revenge on his brother Joe, who arrested him. In a gun battle Joe kills Rico and mourns the loss.

The basic plot outline belies the extraordinary amount of detail and backstory that Pat Mills crammed into six pages. Up to Prog 30, Dredd's background had been restricted, so Mills set about correcting this deficiency and came up with the seminal evolution of Dredd's character: "After ROBOT WARS, John Wagner took Dredd back, and I kind of left it with him until he ran out of time and asked me to do two filler Dredd stories. I wrote THE NEON KNIGHTS [Prog 29 – a story based upon the post-ROBOT WARS rise of a Klan-style mob, with robots replacing Negro slaves] and THE RETURN OF RICO."

It was the latter story that Mills was particularly proud of: "I really wanted to write a carefully planned and very powerful story that was truly special. I spent two days walking around trying to search my psyche to come up with a plot, then suddenly this idea hit me, it came from nowhere. Looking back maybe it was my subconscious trying to awaken my true feelings about Dredd. I had felt many stories I'd written were done strictly by the numbers, but this was completely different. It was not that the story was particularly well-written or drawn but it tapped directly into the human subconscious and dredged up so much pain and doubt, that made it so popular."

The story's popularity was such that *2000 AD* readers voted it the top Dredd story of 1977, and it wasn't just the readers who identified with it, as Kevin O'Neill readily admits: "I loved the first spark of a human side in Dredd that Pat wrote into THE RETURN OF RICO and he continued this theme through THE CURSED EARTH."

It was this spark that Mills knew needed clarifying: "All the time on Dredd, I was always searching to humanise him. Partly, because he had already lost his original take – namely, he couldn't shoot people for dropping litter, so we ended up with an uneasy compromise. Was he a hero or was he a bastard? This has always been a problem over the years. Some may say this dichotomy makes him an interesting character. I feel it's more of an inconsistency, which none of us – writers or artists – has been happy about. It means you are not sure what he is. You have to signpost the reader as to your intention – is he good or bad? To this day, nobody is really sure what side of the fence he's on. In the movie, he's a hero, but really we all know Dredd is a complete fascist bastard.

"My problem was – how do I show some humanity in Dredd? The result of this search for Dredd's human side had a simple answer – let's have his brother have the humanity. He's got what Dredd hasn't."

Mills vividly recalls the first image: "I started off with this foul-looking character coming through Customs [see right] claiming he was Judge Dredd and the whole story literally just formed in my mind."

*[Below] Call of the Wilde: Rico has nothing to declare except his genes...*

It is typical of Mills's story-telling style, that he takes three pages (half the strip) to reveal the key element of the story (and Dredd's whole history): that Rico is Dredd's cloned brother. [See above left]

Despite the fact that the Dredd twins were specially and identically cloned to be Judges, Mills twice makes the point that Rico is better than Joe (the classic evil being stronger than the good). This leads onto the major plot point in the story – soon after graduation Joe (the good side) arrests Rico (his dark side) for bribery and murder, as Mills explains: "Rico is everything that Judge Dredd says is not possible in a human psyche. Dredd is saying '*I am all good, I am all perfect, I am wonderful*' – but he's a human being and that's not possible. If he is doing all those good things what's happened to his dark side? It's gone – into his brother – who turns out to be a very tragic character, paying for Dredd's holier-than-thou attitude.

"It may seem on the surface to be a revenge story with Rico criticising the straight Dredd – but underneath lurks the classic mythological dark twin duality conflict. I felt that not even Dredd could be that good or noble – never taking a bribe, totally incorruptible. Not even Mother Theresa is that perfect. And as such, perfection must be made to pay a price. Everyone has another side to their character, evil has its good side – even Hitler loved dogs!

"The heart of the Rico story is that it reveals the latent dark side of Dredd, the side he is unwilling to face up to or show himself. The fact that Rico can accept his dark side (which becomes projected onto Dredd) fuels the hatred between the two even more."

Dredd's actions reveal that the Judge System is his true family. No one is above the law, not even one's own bloodline. This blind faith to the Justice System and its suspect past is what finally cemented Dredd's character for the years to come.

Once transported to Titan, a moon with little atmosphere and a gravity far less than Earth, Rico's face is customised to fit his new environment [see above right]. The resulting face is similar to that of Al Rico from *Action*'s 'Death Race 1999'. Mills denies any direct link: "As for my Rico looking similarly ugly to the 'Death Game' Rico, we were very fond of making people look as ugly and foul as possible. Unless Mike McMahon used 'Death Game' as a reference, I think we just decided to make him look absolutely disgusting. So we had this vicarious thrill of this monster *claiming* to be Judge Dredd. We knew, in comics, that anyone who'd had major facial surgery was popular, it would be like saying weird robots were popular."

### NATURAL CLONED KILLERS

As well as creating Dredd's birth and childhood, Mills became the first writer to give Dredd a first name - Joe. Coincidentally, 'Death Game 1999' (from *Action*) had a story where the hero JOE Taggart has a long running feud with a facially-scarred cyborg called Al RICO, which ended in a bloody feud to the end [see left]. Mills claims no direct connection between the two sets of names: "I'm very fond of the name Joe - my character in 'Marshal Law' [for Epic Comics] is also called Joe, don't ask me why...there's also Joe Pineapples [from Mills's 'ABC Warriors' in *2000 AD*].

"As for Rico, I wasn't consciously aware of 'Death Game'. I was after a name synonymous with corruption, the Mafia, and that sort of character, which is where I got the name Rico from."

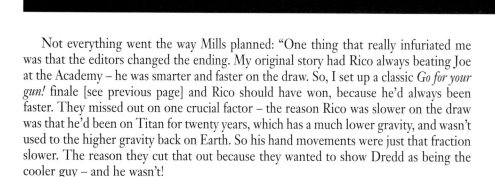

Joe may be a common name but it does crop up with alarming regularity in other Mills's comics and stories, as well as the ones mentioned above, for example: "Scarface" Joe Levine (THE NEW YOU) and Joe Brontowski (from Mills's 'Flesh' strip in *2000 AD*). Also note, in *Battle*, Mills's Rat Pack leader was a Major Taggart.

Not everything went the way Mills planned: "One thing that really infuriated me was that the editors changed the ending. My original story had Rico always beating Joe at the Academy – he was smarter and faster on the draw. So, I set up a classic *Go for your gun!* finale [see previous page] and Rico should have won, because he'd always been faster. They missed out on one crucial factor – the reason Rico was slower on the draw was that he'd been on Titan for twenty years, which has a much lower gravity, and wasn't used to the higher gravity back on Earth. So his hand movements were just that fraction slower. The reason they cut that out because they wanted to show Dredd as being the cooler guy – and he wasn't!

"When I think about it, RICO was an attack on Dredd, not in a subversive way, it's an interaction in story terms that exposes some of the weaknesses in Dredd. By changing the ending, they actually covered them up. I was very cross with them for doing that."

Mills was happy with one part of his ending: "I did manage to get that wonderful line in from the Hollies' pop song. It seemed so deliciously appropriate. I wanted to take the piss out of Dredd, the amused cynicism that is the trademark of Dredd anyway, as well as showing the love for his brother. It all worked so well." [See page opposite]

Mills's final words neatly sum up his own single seminal episode: "*It all worked so well.*" Mills had given Dredd a past, and a hell of a past at that! The psychological undertones that swept through the strip reverberated around the Dredd strip for many

years to come, with a number of influential stories being written based on this one episode. But the biggest tribute to Mills's creativity was that the movie used this scenario as the basis for its own story, as David Bishop relates: "Although it was only six pages – it's a major story. It introduces Rico, a major villain in the film and sets up one of the key plot elements in the movie.

Bishop continues: "In terms of Dredd in the comic it showed Dredd wasn't just a cop, he had a life outside. It was a major turning point in Dredd because it does start to show other aspects of his character – the fact that he makes a moral decision, having had to make a moral decision in the past. The arrest of his brother, so soon after graduation, hardened him as a person and, more importantly, as a Judge. I don't think the significance of it was grasped fully at the time. It is truly a classic story and wasted in six pages, which is why Pat is saving himself to write a new Rico story for *2000 AD*."

The original RICO story led to a number of later episodes which drew on the same central theme of the two sides of Dredd's character, but RICO has its greatest influence in a nine-year-long central theme that is covered in greater detail in Chapters 25 to 27.

## KEEPING DREDD'S HATTON!

**Another important aspect of the Dredd legend that is clearly revealed in THE RETURN OF RICO is his face. Despite elaborate efforts, over the years, never to show Dredd's face, it is revealed twice in this one strip.**

**Firstly in the firing range scene, both Joe and Rico are shown without their helmets, albeit in profile - importantly, both are identical looking. A few frames later, when Rico has been arrested, he reveals a full face and, therefore, if they are identical, Joe's face.** Mills's recollections are not conclusive: "It probably wasn't a deliberate process to show the face, although I must have thought about it to write it in."

Back in the days of Jack Adrian's aborted COURTROOM script the principle of not showing Dredd's face had obviously not been a major concern: "No one told me not to show his face. That was something that was gradually built up over the years, I suppose. There was no deliberate covering up of Dredd's face from the start."

But the covering of Dredd's face became an early element in the strip:

In ANTIQUE CAR HEIST (Prog 8), Massimo Belardinelli drew Dredd taking off his helmet and revealing his face but editorial staff "Censored" it. [See page 56 for picture]

In THE FACE-CHANGERS (Prog 52), Dredd's face is seen in full but has been face-changed to lawyer Manny Bloom. The "face" is that of 1940s Hollywood actor Rondo Hatton. [See left].

**In THE NEW LAW (Prog 90), Dredd is seen on his sickbed, naked except for bandages round his face - which reveal his eyes [see right]. Similar bandaged Dredd heads were drawn in DEATH CRAWL (Prog 85) and HITMAN (Progs 571-573) - which revealed more face than before.**

During THE APOCALYPSE WARS (Progs 245-270), the Sov-Cit Judges took Dredd's helmet off, revealing black hair on the back of his head - but no full frontal. For THE SHOOTING PARTY (Prog 515), John Cooper recalls: "I was tempted to draw in his face but in the end all you see is the back of his head when he swings down on the vine. When he is *seen* front on, I drew the top half in silhouette."

But even this restricted view [see right] proved too revealing, so art assistant Kevin Brighton was called on to draw vine leaves to obscure the back of Dredd's head: "His hair was black and cropped short before I covered it up."

IN THE BATH (Prog 626). While Dredd is 'seen' taking a bath, he makes a double arrest in his flat, without showing his face - or leaving his bath. Jim Baikie (who also drew HITMAN above) tells how he managed to keep Dredd's face off-frame: "I had to show his head cropped by the panel border to the exact amount that it would have been obscured by his helmet - and viewed from the back. A loofah with the arm down his back allowed the same amount of concealment that his helmet would have done. God knows what sort of head and face he would have, because we only ever show his chin and the tip of his nose. In the story, Dredd's got a dimple, and has three days stubbly growth of whiskers - the same as I had when I looked in the shaving mirror."

John Wagner owns up to the inspiration behind this story: "I wrote it in the bath. Sometimes I'd take a pad in with me and just relax and write notes, whatever comes into my head. The water was probably very cold before it was finished."

Never revealing Dredd's face is something that those who have worked on the strip have defended with all their might and creative power, Wagner being the most vociferous: "We had to resist demands to see his face from so many quarters, but in a way it sums up the facelessness of justice – justice has no soul. So it isn't necessary for readers to see Dredd's face, and I don't want you to."

Brian Bolland agrees with Wagner: "I don't think we should ever see his face – I mean, the fact that no one knows for sure what he looks like adds greatly to his mystique. However, that all depends on John Wagner – if he decides to show us Dredd underneath that helmet, then it's okay with me."

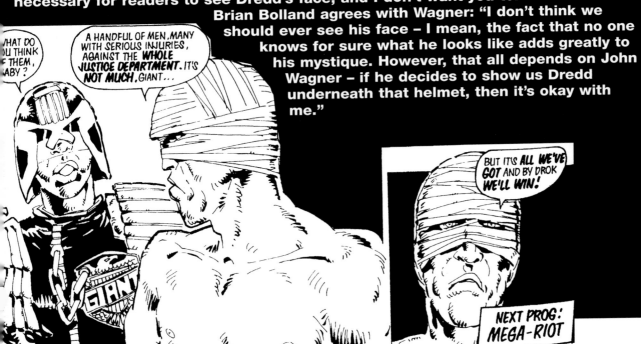

DREDD

### MUTIE THE PIG (Prog 34)
*Writer:* John Wagner
*Artists:* Mike McMahon and Ian Gibson
     *PLOT:* Dredd fakes his own funeral in order to uncover a corrupt
     Judge – his close friend Judge Gibson.

This story could be loosely classed as John Wagner's sequel to Pat Mills's RETURN OF RICO, since it develops Mills's dark side of the law concept even further. Wagner has Dredd echoing his own words from RICO: "*A bent judge is the worst kind of criminal.*" But the two writers should have spoken to each other because some glaring continuity errors appear... The pic [see right] almost left Pat Mills, for once, speechless: "Dredd and therefore Rico were born in 2066 and graduated in 2079 [from Prog 27] aged thirteen. [Wagner's ACADEMY OF LAW states graduation at age twenty] I think we'll have to say, they both had genetically accelerated developments...or they were born seven years old, or something. In the case of Joe and Rico, they were genetically created to be Judges...more the way things are these days. It's not like the years of searching for the next Dalai Lama, Judges are created in a laboratory. These are guys who don't even sleep....or have nookie – no wonder Dredd's so fucking miserable."

Dredd is seen erasing Gibson's name from Roll of Honour, as he had done with Rico's name, but looking at the Roll of Honour (page 69) there is no sign of any space where Rico's name would have been.

Someone else erased in this strip was Judge Gibson, as Ian Gibson (the artist) freely admits: "Mike McMahon drew the first episode of MUTIE THE PIG and made Judge Gibson out to be a spiky haired-character, not like me at all, I came in on the second episode and had the pleasure of killing myself off."

*TRIVIA NOTE: Judge Hunt was killed in MEGA-CITY 5000 (Prog 41), while no trace of Judge Wagner's demise has been recorded. It is quite possible that Judge Wagner never appeared other than as a name on the Honour Roll.*

"In ACADEMY OF LAW, I'd come up with the names on Dredd's Roll of Honour for the class of 2079 – Wagner, Gibson and Hunt [but no Rico!]. John decided that we were not allowed to get away with that and that the names had to be killed off."

Not content with letting Pat Mills give Dredd a first name, in RETURN OF RICO, Wagner comes up with Dredd's Academy nickname – Old Stoney Face. Again, continuity falls down because in later stories the name is sometimes spelt Stony.

Interestingly, up to this point in Dredd's development, his three most memorable enemies (other than Call-Me-Kenneth and the revolting robots) were: Rico (his brother), Gibson (his best friend) and even, the self-styled, Whitey – all Judges, in some form. Dredd's most formidable foes had all come from within the Judge System – which confirmed the Judges' importance and enforced Dredd's total psychological devotion to his profession.

This injudicious trend of bad Judges continued in later stories with Dredd pitted against the likes of Judge Cal, Judge Death, the Dark Judges, et al...

### MEGA-CITY 5000 Pt 2 (Prog 41)
*Writer:* John Wagner
*Artist:* Brian Bolland
> PLOT: Dredd puts an end to an illegal motorbike race between the Spacers and Muties.

This story, influenced by the inspirational *Death Race 2000* movie, is important for the introduction of two names into the Dredd history books: artist Brian Bolland and Mutie biker "Spikes" Harvey Rotten, who dies in the last frame.

In his debut Dredd strip [see left] Bolland closely copied a Mike McMahon lorry (from Prog 18 – see page 68) for his opening frame. It is this extreme eye for accuracy and detail that was to become Bolland's trademark, as Kevin O'Neill eulogises: "Of the few Dredds he drew, Bolland romanticised Dredd and attracted many followers as a result. Which is why in a lot of people's eyes he is the definitive Dredd artist.

"McMahon and Carlos were both scruffier than Bolland and they made Dredd look meaner and more brutal. Bolland's art was clean and beautiful, enabling him to get away with the violence. Whereas McMahon suffered the fall-out because it looks grittier and scruffier, so it attracted more complaints from the powers that be."

Bolland recalls his Dredd debut: "Dave Gibbons and I had worked on a Nigerian *Powerman* comic and met Kelvin Gosnell before the launch of *2000 AD*, who showed us preliminary artwork and strips. Soon after, Dave was taken on to draw the first 'Harlem Heroes', and I stayed with *Powerman* for a few months.

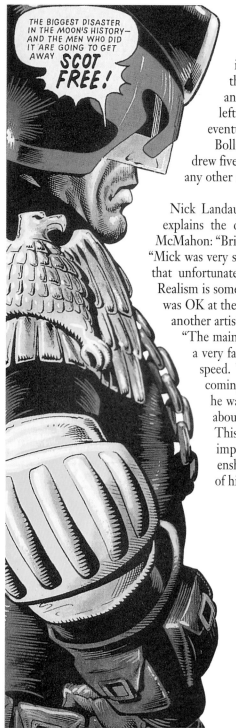

THE BIGGEST DISASTER IN THE MOON'S HISTORY— AND THE MEN WHO DID IT ARE GOING TO GET AWAY *SCOT FREE!*

"I did buy the new mag, except the very first issue which sold out before I could get one. I saw the Dredd story as just another new comic story and didn't think much about it. It was after Kelvin left *2000 AD* to launch *Starlord*, that Nick Landau eventually asked me to do my first Dredd story."

Bolland (modest to a fault) fails to mention that he drew five of the first twenty *2000 AD* covers – more than any other artist.

Nick Landau, the man who brought Bolland onto Dredd explains the differences between the new artist and Mike McMahon: "Brian drew in a much more realistic style."[See left] "Mick was very stylised [see below right] and to a certain extent that unfortunately made him less popular with the readers." Realism is something the kids always love. Brian's first artwork was OK at the time, it wasn't the greatest. But then Brian was another artist who developed in leaps and bounds.

"The main difference between the two was that Mick was a very fast artist and Brian was slow – legendary for his speed. You knew when you saw a page of Brian's art coming in that it would be a near perfect page, because he was someone who would go away and think about things."

This creative thinking time was very important to Bolland, who enshrined himself in one frame of his first strip:

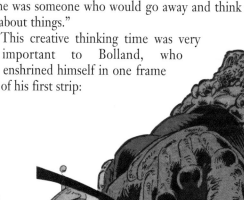

IN ORBIT EVERY MONDAY

"Having worked very closely with Dave Gibbons on many projects, we had nicknames for each other – Gibbo and Bollo. So, I put my nickname on a woman's shopping bag as the bikers roar past. It was easier than thinking up new names. I was slow enough in meeting deadlines, without having to think up new names all the time."

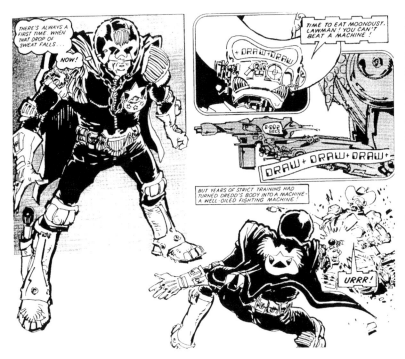

In the dark, distant days of Dredd's development, Pat Mills sought but failed to locate the new wave of British artists, who would replace the old-school of aged British and Argentinian artists. During this next period of growth and development (Progs 42-85), three young artists – Mike McMahon, Brian Bolland and Ian Gibson – monopolised the artwork and all three would collaborate on Wagner's second saga...

### LUNA PERIOD (Progs 42-59)
*Writer:* John Wagner
*Artists:* Ian Gibson, Mike McMahon and Brian Bolland

*PLOT:* This was Wagner's second episodic series, after ROBOT WARS, with Dredd transferred to the moon for a six-month stint as Judge Marshal of Luna-1.

Having changed Dredd's location, Wagner decided to change his uniform – an attempt to change his character, possibly a decision that harked back to his dislike of Ezquerra's original uniform. The editorial team were less than happy with Wagner's apparent mood swings, as Kevin O'Neill attests: "There was a period early on where there was a lot of moaning going on. John was not happy about Dredd and insisted he wore a cape and anti-gravity boots [see above left] – we didn't like the idea but he was adamant. Of course, when he saw them, he demanded the capes be whited out. We told him to fuck off and left them in. John learnt to leave the uniform alone after that."

It was at this time (Prog 44), that O'Neill drew the first Dredd front cover since Prog 18, which again suggests the low esteem the strip was still held within the comic.

Brian Bolland drew his second Dredd strip (LAND RACE Prog 47), and was less than happy with being lumped with a new format: "I hated the idea of those double-page

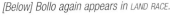

*[Below] Bollo again appears in LAND RACE.*

opening spreads. It didn't work at all well from an artistic point of view. I'm not very good at crowd scenes or all that epic stuff. I prefer to do more close-up action and intimate detail, with one or two figures. When I was given this first one, I thought, '*Christ! what on earth am I to do?*'"

In Prog 50 Wagner introduced the Sov-Blok Judges [see right], revealing for the first time that the Judge System was a global concept. In the years to come Judges from all around the world cropped up, each with their own "traditional" uniform.

Toward the end of this Luna series, it became apparent that Wagner's sharpness was getting blunted, as Nick Landau notes: "John was getting a little tired of writing Dredd. There was something lacking in his Moon stories like ELVIS – THE KILLER CAR, it was getting twee, soft – not even very funny."

As Landau suggests, Wagner had got a little soft, and the acting editor knew a change was necessary: "It was Pat Mills's suggestion to harden Dredd's image – give him that edge. When the first CURSED EARTH script hit the office it was like a lightning bolt. Here was the new Judge Dredd, and in many ways that is what defined the Judge Dredd of today. All the stories up till then were not really the Judge that we know now. That's why Pat would say it was the Golden Age because it was the new beginning for Dredd."

### THE CURSED EARTH (Progs 61-85)

*"It remains the most ambitious Judge Dredd story yet conceived. Twenty-five episodes and over one hundred and fifty pages of artwork is all the more remarkable for the fact that only two artists – Mike McMahon and Brian Bolland – worked on it."*
Nick Landau – December 1981
*Writers:* Pat Mills (John Wagner and Jack Adrian)
*Artists:* Mike McMahon and Brian Bolland

> PLOT: With Mega-City Two, on the US western seaboard, in the grip of a plague, Dredd volunteers to deliver the life-saving serum. With his team of three Judges, war droids and a punk-biker "Spikes" Harvey Rotten, Dredd travels across the Cursed Earth in an impregnable combi-assault vehicle.
>
> On the way, they do battle with an odd assortment of characters – Killer Flying Rats, the Brotherhood of Muties, Robot-Vampires, Slay-Riders, Burger Barons, Dinosaurs, Las Vegas Mafia Judges and Berserker War Droids, before the destination is reached.

Having written the most popular Dredd story of 1977 (THE RETURN OF RICO), Pat Mills's next Dredd story was voted the most popular of 1978. Whereas RICO defined Dredd's geminic-genesis and psychological piece of mind, THE CURSED EARTH blew open the physical and philosophical side to his nature.

It was this evolutionary extension of Dredd's personality, through Mills's superlative story-telling combined with two young artists given the time and space to quickly develop into twin artistic legends, that made THE CURSED EARTH the most important and influential Dredd saga ever. McMahon and Bolland both complemented Mills's epic storyline with some alveolar-busting artwork that would leave a hyper-ventilating lung-fish breathless.

Among Bolland's unforgettable images is the simple I AM THE LAW scene which defines Dredd's philosophical megamorphosis, as Nick Landau, who commissioned the saga, explains: "During the journey, Dredd underwent a complete character change – from a relentless, macho cop, who could cope with the insanity of Mega-City One by being tougher and more ruthless than its inhabitants, to a fairer, more compassionate lawman whose treatment of the Cursed Earth mutants was both sympathetic and just."

To evaluate the story's importance in detail would take up this whole book, so the following few features have been chosen to give as complete a picture behind the saga as space allows...

With John Wagner becoming a little moonstruck with his lengthy LUNA series, Landau handed over the keys of Mega-City One to Mills, who unlocked the city gates and Dredd's psyche – as well as his own.

Mills knew he had to look beyond the confines of the City: "John [who wrote all twenty-three stories between RICO and CURSED EARTH] and I were quite respectful of each other's Dredd stories and characters, so we generally stayed away from them.

"For me MC1 had become claustrophobic and a character as large as Dredd needed a bigger canvas to work on. I felt there were certain things we could do outside the Mega-City, which had become a little stultifying. In THE CURSED EARTH, I suddenly found time and space for pre-history, further development and to include some missing elements. I thought where are the mutants from films like *The Omega Man*? Where is that *Dark Rain* type of story about pollution wars? We needed a strange landscape to offset the City.

"Above all, we wanted some bloody aliens. It had been in my mind, from the very start of *2000 AD*, that we should have every kind of fantasy genre imaginable. Aliens, robots, mutants – all the things that hadn't been represented in the comic up till then should feature in THE CURSED EARTH. Many of my new ideas, features and characters were never again seen in MC1."

As with THE RETURN OF RICO, the focal point of this journey was Mills's own desire for back-story: "My logic behind THE CURSED EARTH was to discover the history of the Judges – I had to know why characters are the way they are and where they came from. But when I started to write it, I got totally carried away with the sheer size of it all and the only thing that stopped me turning it into a fifty-week saga was that we were about to merge with *Starlord* and the saga had to end. I had all these extra stories planned – even one set in the Grand Canyon.

*[Left] McMahon opened the saga with his scrotum-wrenching cover (Prog 61) - which has more balls than the National Lottery and as many imitators.*

"I had become very passionate about what was basically a story of oppression, touching a lot of areas where Western civilisation had oppressed other races. It made me feel very angry, I was surprised at the passion I got into the stories, and I like to think, it was this passion that the readers hooked on to."

To capture the emotional theme and struggle of "the oppressed citizen", one new character Mills brought into the saga was the super-intelligent alien Tweak [see left], as Nick Landau suggests: "Tweak was an original. Mills had never felt happy writing Walter the Wobot – Dredd's regular companion – and wanted a character that the readers could sympathise with. One that could get beaten up, tortured and shot at – yet still come out alive!"

Despite Landau's claims of authenticity, Mills's alien inspiration was soon uncovered in the *2000 AD* letters page...

> *Dear Tharg,*
> *I have a complaint to make. The alien Tweak is not an alien at all, but a tamandua, or clawed anteater. I saw a picture of one in* National Geographic, *where it was stated that this tamandua could step straight into a science-fiction film – or even a comic perhaps?*
> *J.F. Garner, Beaconsfield, Bucks*

The spark that ignited Mills's imagination for the epic journey was, in his own words, quite simple: "I'd heard about *Damnation Alley*, I'm not sure about the film, but certainly the book [by Roger Zelazny] was out. So, I decided to do something like it. It was a conscious decision on our part not to use the essence of *Damnation Alley* but to use that kind of generic road-movie concept as a framework to give us a direction."

Mills's saga reversed the Trans-American journey of the *Damnation Alley* story and mirrored other key elements, as Paul Taylor's film review in *Time Out* suggests: "A post-holocaust [read Atomic Wars] odyssey tracks an amphibious armoured truck [multi-assault vehicle] from a California missile base [Mega-City One] cross-country [Cursed Earth] towards signs of life in Albany, New York [Mega-City Two]. A military redneck [Judge] and a rebel [punk-biker] gather a model post-nuclear family – one black, one woman, one kid – [one alien] like tokens en route hampered by derivative confrontations with mutant mountain men [muties] and man-eating cockroaches [robot-vampires]."

Whatever its sources, the saga unveiled a new art-layout, as Roy Preston explains: "With the success of Dredd, two new styles were combined in THE CURSED EARTH to open each episode – a full double-page spread of one single pic, in colour. Since this was Dredd's first epic saga, it needed to be treated in a fresh way.

"Pat welcomed this new trend – all he had to write for the first two pages of most strips was, say, '*Dredd crossing the Cursed Earth*' and leave the rest up to the artist's imagination."

Preston outlines how the two artists reacted differently to this new format: "Mike loved the freedom to draw a double-page instead of cramped up frames, and responded with some magnificently imaginative opening spreads – full of impactive, graphic art – that took our breath away."

Jack Adrian has fond memories of a McMahon masterpiece [see right]: "The original artwork now hangs on my wall at home. Mike gave it to me as a gift, because I kept going on in the pub about it. I still think it's the most wonderful opening splash – an iconic piece of artwork. The only thing wrong is the dialogue: TWENTY-FIRST CENTURY COP should have read TWENTY-SECOND."

Preston continues: "Brian Bolland was less enthused, but still created his own unique masterpieces."

The MUTIE MOUNTAINS is the one double-spread that Bolland was happy drawing: "The only epic spread I really enjoyed drawing was the Presidents' faces carved in the mountain. That gave me a great chance for close-up detail."

Again, Jack Adrian has a story to tell about this mountainous spread: "Although Pat is not an innocent he used to amaze us with his lack of knowledge, most especially in not knowing where Mount Rushmore National Park was. Having plotted out his story, Pat discovered the actual site was a lot further west than he'd hoped. Not wanting to change the chronology of his story, he simply changed America. He wrote an extra paragraph explaining how Rushmore had been relocated just outside MC1 on the premise that sightseers wouldn't have so far to travel to see it."

As usual, Mills has his own explanation: "I desperately wanted to have this storyline early in the series and found the real Mount Rushmore was too far from New York, so I moved it. It was my attempt to show up American kitsch culture at its most vulgar."

Like the alien Tweak, not all the *new* CURSED EARTH characters and concepts were Mills's originals. He resurrected two characters from previous Wagner stories: Judge Jack (from ROBOT WARS) and, more importantly, "Spikes" Harvey Rotten, as Nick Landau expounds: "Pat pulled Rotten from THE MEGA-CITY 5000 [Progs 41–42], and fleshed out his character, giving him a more appropriate visual appearance."

The inclusion of "Spikes" is important to Mills in softening Dredd's character. The one-dimensional punk-biker doesn't change his spots during the journey and acts as the *voice of the Mega-City* during the trek, best typified through Mills's words and Bolland's artwork [see left].

However, the return of "Spikes" is slightly suspect, since he died at the end of Prog 42. A second continuity cock-up concerning "Spikes" is that Wagner made him the leader of the Mutie Brotherhood, but Mills introduces "Spikes" as knowing "*the Cursed Earth from his days of gun-running to the Muties!*" Mills owns up to both points: "I was as bad as John and never read other people's stories either."

The reason for these oversights can be put down to Mills being more concerned with creating a new definitive backstory. Having uncovered Dredd's past in RICO, Mills set about creating the origins of the Judge System: "I always have to know the history of everything, which is why I wrote the story about President Booth. I just had to know how the Judges came to be." It is typical of Mills's sly humour to name the last American President after Lincoln's assassin.

More importantly, Mills's backstory not only put the Judge System into historical context, but gave the whole Dredd mythos the sort of credible base that has been built upon by other stories ever since, as Dredd himself explains below…

With the saga in full swing – Dredd having seen off Giant Flying Rats, Mutie Mountain Men, saved the President's life and rescued Tweak from the Slay-Riders – Mills's output dropped and gave Nick Landau serious editorial problems: "When Pat started slowing down it was a nightmare putting those stories together. As the colour pages had to go to press two weeks before the black and white, I found myself taking dictation over the phone from Pat, who was working out the story in his head, so a script could go off to Mick or Brian. Pat wouldn't write the black and white pages until a week or two later."

Despite the editorial back-up, Mills continued to miss deadlines, which finally forced Landau's hand: "Writing was powertorial with Pat and John, who, as creators of the comic, got very much their own head on a number of things. It wasn't a case of saying to Pat, '*Look, I'm taking* THE CURSED EARTH *away from you unless you hit deadline*.' It was slightly more subtle, reminding him we were always running very late and we must do something about it. The something was the fill-in stories, which was ironic since these were the ones which became notorious."

Landau commissioned John Wagner and Jack Adrian to do a couple of stories each to help ease Mills's writing load. Neither writer's original strips can be reprinted, and for once it wasn't direct internal interference from the IPC management that canned Dredd stories.

Wagner's two-parter THE BATTLE OF THE BURGER BARONS and BURGER LAW (Progs 71-72) concerned the Kentucky Burger Wars between two rival factions under the leadership of Ronald MacDonald and the Burger King. The use of trademark symbols proved too much for the lawyers of the two burger conglomerates, as were scenes of explicit violence, such as having Ronald shoot one of his staff for not wiping down a table, and boasting "*Everythin' at MacDonalds' is disposable, includin' th' staff!*" Needless to say, the strip was swiftly banned, although it was published in the original *2000 AD*.

The two extra writers allowed Mills to concentrate his efforts on a four-week series, which ran the full gamut of creative emotion. The central character in these episodes being Satanus – a genetically recreated Tyrannosaurus Rex, the offspring of Old One-Eye, a previous Mills creation (first seen in Prog 9 of *2000 AD* in 'Flesh'). Seventeen years after Mills wrote the story, it is interesting to compare his idea of DNA genetic recreation with *Jurassic Park*.

Certain elements of this dinosaur series touched a raw nerve in Mills: "The scene where Satanus (the Devil beast) is perched atop a Mexican church was, for me, deeply symbolic, referring to the forces of evil triumphing over good. A very, very potent image that sent out very, very powerful signals." Jack Adrian confirms this: "Pat was always anti-church, anti-religion – it showed in a lot of his work."

It was Adrian who wrote the next two episodes, GIANTS AREN'T GENTLEMEN and SOUL FOOD (Progs 77-78) – the second batch of stories to be banned due to breaches of copyright law. Again major trademark characters were used in the strip, which helped fulfil a lifelong ambition for Jack Adrian: "I'd always wanted to write a story using lots of advertising icons and characters. I included Colonel Sanders (of Kentucky Fried Chicken fame), Jolly Green Giant, Michelin Man, Tate and Lyle Sugar-Cube Man, and The Alka-Selzer Kid. But after the stories had been published, the Jolly Green Giant people sued IPC who, I believe, made an out of court financial settlement. And my initial two strips were banned from ever being printed again."

Nick Landau explains how the second legal battle was resolved: "It was Kelvin and John Sanders who got round the copyright problem by writing a half-page comic strip retraction in a later issue." [See left]

Mills was none too happy with the four stories written for HIS epic: "Jack Adrian wrote the Jolly Green Giant story because I was having hell's trouble keeping to schedules and couldn't keep up. Nick Landau, who was always looking for a controversial angle, suggested Jack, and I agreed – to allow me to concentrate on the final aspects of the journey. Looking

[Left] Judge Dredd gets himself into a pickle...and a sesame seed bun - in the Burger Wars.

back I believe the Burger wars and jolly green giant strips were a big mistake, and my feeling was that we couldn't get away with it. And we didn't."

With the impending merger of *2000 AD* with its brother comic *Starlord*, Pat Mills was forced to prematurely wrap up his epic journey. But first, two major aspects of the story needed to be sorted out: "I felt "Spikes" needed to die to create a real sense of drama as Dredd crawled, alone, on his knees toward Mega-City Two. Only one man was going to get through this nuclear hell. And that came over pretty well – he really was crawling at the end, all these things were coming back and beating the shit out of him, he had to shoot himself in the leg to get through – he had to do the fucking lot. [See right]

"In the end, you get these feeling of '*wow!* what a hero', and I think in this instance he, unashamedly, was a hero. I couldn't have written the story any other way – the cold, merciless Dredd of the Mega-City streets couldn't have made that journey. The city was about control, THE CURSED EARTH was about lack of control – it brought out the different halves of Dredd's psyche."

The penultimate word on this epic struggle both on and off the page is left to Nick Landau: "Putting it together, week after week, felt like we were actually crossing the Cursed Earth just to do it. What with writer and artist delays, plus the need to get a comic out every week – it was a trek, in itself. It was a totally new experience – it was so good it could have been Judge Dredd number one."

By the end of THE CURSED EARTH, Pat Mills (who had taken a year to pre-define Dredd's original character) had managed to streamline it sympathetically and, just as vitally, defined the concept of the Judge System – which had been such a key element to the very first Dredd story – JUDGE WHITEY. This saga and THE RETURN OF RICO act as the two definitive stories which set up Dredd – the character and the strip – for the years ahead.

With the character and strip now fully fleshed out, and a runaway success, Mills relinquished control of Dredd and left him to his creator: "Dredd went back to John, who had only been expecting a short break, but found himself sitting out for twenty-five weeks. He was always going through these phases of losing interest in a character but then wanting it back."

Wagner's comments on the saga, although short, are to the point: "It was a bloody good story – broad in scope, imaginative, fast-paced. Which just about sums it up." When Wagner finally got Dredd back, he rejoined a merged comic. On 14 October 1978, *2000 AD* (Prog 86) absorbed *Starlord* – its glossier, more expensive, and better selling IPC clone.

Dave Gibbons's front cover [see right] gave top billing to Judge Dredd (strip written by Wagner and drawn by Bolland), over the other three stories: *2000 AD*'s 'Flesh' (Preston and Belardinelli) and from *Starlord* – 'Strontium Dog' (Wagner and Ezquerra) and 'Ro-Busters' (Mills and Gibbons).

With a new merged comic and following the triumph of THE CURSED EARTH, Nick Landau recalls the way forward: "Dredd's personality, what little of it there is, was developed by Pat during THE CURSED EARTH. His character was much better defined by Pat and I think it had a profound influence on John Wagner, because he could see how the character could be developed. John actually had more of an American comics background because he'd been brought up in the States and had got into the British comic habit of one-off stories and a few multiple-parters. But after Pat wrote THE CURSED EARTH it inspired John to get really cracking and get on with JUDGE CAL."

# THE ART OF THE POSSIBLE

> "The JUDGE CAL saga is far too long. There's about ninety-nine different artists in it and some of it looks decidedly ropey."
>
> *DAVID BISHOP – MARCH 1995*

**The JUDGE CAL saga** (Progs 86-108)
*Writer*: John Wagner
*Artists*: Mike McMahon, Brendan McCarthy, Brett Ewins, Brian Bolland, Garry Leach, Ron Smith and Dave Gibbons

*PLOT*: Crazed dictator Judge Cal seizes power and exerts a hundred-day reign of terror over Mega-City One in which millions of citizens die. Dredd is framed for murder but escapes to overthrow Cal with the help of loyal Judges and city outcast Fergee.

[Above] Dredd is framed for murder in CRIME AND PUNISHMENT [Prog 86] in a scene copied in the movie.

Known popularly as JUDGE CAL, this saga comprises three introductory stories (on the framing of Dredd for a murder actually committed by Cal's 'Dredd' robot) and the twenty-part mini-series THE DAY THE LAW DIED. This was the first epic based in Mega-City One, allowing John Wagner to further flesh out the city and the Judge System. The Academy of Law is expanded upon, illustrating the sheer enormity of the judicial operation and the story introduces Judge Fargo – the Father of Justice...and more besides. Judge Giant is enhanced as a black hero, super-cool and hip, a virtual "friend" of Dredd, proving that other Judges need not be merely faceless supporting characters to JD.

JUDGE CAL provides a major personal turning point for Dredd, both in the comic strip and the movie, as David Bishop points out: "Initially Dredd accepts his sentence for murder. But he comes to his senses, as he realises the law is not infallible, because a miscarriage of justice has occurred – to him – and he decides to fight to free his name."

The saga also provides another key name in the movie, Dredd's Joe Pesci-type sidekick – Fergee. But, as Bishop reveals: "The film's Fergee bears no resemblance to the comic Fergee [see above], who is a baseball bat-swinging country bumpkin who inhabits the sewers."

As well as confirming his psychological growth, Dredd's position within the Judge System is also reaffirmed. He may be the most able and feared Judge on patrol, but he eventually refuses the position of Chief Judge: "*My place is where it has always been. On the streets...I am needed there more than ever now.*"

JUDGE CAL also points towards the growing sophistication of Wagner's storylines. This was not just an action-adventure story transposed from THE CURSED EARTH, it is Wagner's study in the politics of madness, a graphic portrayal of how insane dictators like Cal pervert government, justice and the law. Wagner drew comparisons between Cal and Hitler just as he had done in the ROBOT WARS with Call-Me-Kenneth and the Nazi Führer. This is advanced for a late-1970s boys' comic, but as Roy Preston observes: "During JUDGE CAL, *2000 AD* ceased to be primarily aimed at the normal comic age-range of seven to twelve. It appealed to a much more mature market, although its original readership still identified with the strong action element. At one time we were selling 200,000 copies per issue, which proved how well the new format worked."

But perhaps more important than Wagner's oft-stated political undertones is the wildly inconsistent art which ironically set a precedent for the look of the Dredd strip for the future. JUDGE CAL revealed that Judge Dredd was still in its visual puberty. The strip acted as a melting pot of ideas with artists working out their own personal look for Dredd and his world. It stands as a blueprint for the best aspects of Dredd to come – the energy born of artistic freedom which leaps off the page, but it also has its side-effects – an absence of continuity!

The Dredd strip had quickly become a victim of its ambitions. Because of its drive for bigger and better epic stories spanning six months, the strip was storing up man-management problems which would plague editors for years to come. It was a matter of bad-timing – JUDGE CAL followed hard on the heels of THE CURSED EARTH. John Wagner was back and clearly intent on stamping his authority after the previous Pat Mills dominated opus. This left Steve MacManus, who had taken over as editor, with an emperor-sized headache. Star performers Mike McMahon and Brian Bolland were exhausted after completing THE CURSED EARTH and their order books were just too full with work on covers and annuals to take on another major work as a duo.

This forced MacManus's hand and he gave five new Dredd artists 'try-outs' on this high profile epic. The result was a magnificent coming together of seven artists to work on Wagner's homage to *I, Claudius*. However, this nightmare of artistic co-ordination resulted in a work which often appears more reminiscent of "Carry On Up Pompeii"!

Dredd changed appearance from week to week. Even details such as the eye-slots in his helmet, substitute eyes in effect, varied widely from squinting, narrow slits to a pop-eyed surprised look. Wagner's blockbuster return is a patchwork quilt of wild artistic inconsistency, but the writer remains sanguine: "It was a tremendous load for anyone to take on. If we'd had a couple of core artists it might have been better, but artists have their lives and they come and go like anyone. It's difficult, you can't really plan on having the same people for twelve months."

[Below] Two heads are better than one [Prog 88]. In keeping with a traditional theme, Dredd is faced by an identical-looking enemy – in this case Cal's Dredd-robot which perpertrated the murders, Dredd was framed for. Again, the greatest threat to Dredd....is Dredd himself. When he overcomes this self-test, he further reinforces his own character.

Even the basic look of Judge Cal caused problems for the normally precise Brian Bolland, who had the task of creating the look of title character: "In his visual guidelines, John made reference to John Hurt's Caligula in *I, Claudius*, but I didn't have a TV at the time and hadn't seen him in this role. So I based him on John Hurt's role as Quentin Crisp in *The Naked Civil Servant* [see left], which I had seen."

Jack Adrian puts Bolland's Cal into context: "With his long, flowing hair, Cal was clearly based on Pat Mills – who had long red hair! It was an act of pure revenge on Brian's part, using his art, to get his own back on Pat – who was such a control freak. Pat had to have his finger on everything and Brian really got pissed off. Pat would often ring Brian, agonise over artwork and use up Brian's valuable time. They normally got on like a house on fire, but it all got too much for Brian and that's why he drew Cal to look like Pat. Mills was furious when he found out and had Cal's look changed as explained in the frame [see below left]. It was hilariously funny to all of us in the know at the time."

The experiences of the artists involved in JUDGE CAL serve as an illustration to the visual evolution of Dredd in his adolescence. Ron Smith, an artist who already had twenty-four years of experience under his pen for the more tightly controlled American comics where continuity is king, received a shock when he started out on Dredd: "I was sent refs for drawing Dredd, but no two were the same! There was no model sheet for Dredd; there still isn't one, even today. This is no criticism, in fact it was what attracted me to the strip."

Smith proudly recalls his debut [see below]: "They needed somebody who could draw action. After THE CURSED EARTH, we were back in Mega-City One, with vehicles tearing about the place, street fights, lots of secondary characters – it was goodbye to the furry animals!"

This situation inevitably led to anomalies, but none more extreme than the little confession Mike McMahon made to Ron Smith: "Mike told me he'd spent four months drawing Dredd as a black man – which in retrospect is obvious – just look at the mouth and facial lines of his early Dredd's. Whereas Brian and myself had been drawing him as a white man. That was typical of *2000 AD*; other Fleetway comics were so rigidly controlled, yet they let this outfit do what the hell they bloody well liked!"

Eighteen years on this revelation comes as a shock to Dredd debutant Brett Ewins: "Even after all these years of drawing Dredd, I never realised that he could possibly be black. Although it does make sense – I always wondered why McMahon insisted on giving him this particular look. I just copied it, thinking it was just a development of Carlos's creation."

For a character with no face, Dredd's physical stance, his uniform and particulary his helmet were of paramount importance to the artists as they strove to achieve a strong visual identity for him. They did not speak with the same voice, as Kelvin Gosnell observes: "Everyone drew the helmet a different way. Carlos's original concept was based on an American motorcycle cop's, which curves in at the back, but others tended to draw it much straighter."

Brian Bolland had his own ideas: "I had always thought that Carlos's helmet was all wrong. It should have been more parabolic, not fully enclosed." [See right]

Another new Dredd artist on this saga, Brendan McCarthy is also a follower of the new look: "The major change I made to the look of Dredd was the shape of his helmet – giving him a more samurai type of flared helmet rather than Ezquerra's more traditional enclosed bike helmet."

Brett Ewins also has claims on Dredd's uniform [see right]: "I redefined Dredd's helmet, making it sharper, mainly around the eyes and visor. I also made his eagle shoulder pad much more streamlined (and realistic) – a style which was copied by many artists who followed me."

It would be wrong to think of the artists going totally off on their own tangents. Occasionally discussions would take place to "iron" out visual problems, as Smith remembers: "Brian and I discussed how many of the futuristic elements of Dredd originated and how they functioned. We worked out what Dredd's eagle shoulder pad was made of. Mike was convinced it was cast in iron, but we decided it was stuffed and stitched to the suit like his left shoulder pad, so when he turned his shoulder, the wings would follow."

As Smith continues: "Dredd presented a unique problem for us artists, he was literally one among thousands of identical Judges roaming the streets of MC1. Unlike any other character in comics Dredd doesn't have a uniform of his own, he was dressed like any other street Judge, only the name on his badge differentiated him. But you could only see that in close-up, and certainly not if he turned away. He wasn't taller or bigger than the other Judges, but by the end of 1979 you could differentiate him, through his posture and stance. We created this individuality – the classic Dredd pose – legs apart, hands tucked into his body belt. It wasn't in the script, it was an evolutionary process you pick up from a change in another artist's work, and you think 'that works' and progress from there."

Differences in artistic interpretation also extended as far as the depiction of Mega-City One, as Smith also explains: "Mike drew buildings with GI helmets on top, Brian's were taller versions of the New York skyscrapers of today, whereas mine were a blend of the two styles." McMahon agrees: "I had a distinctive idea of how it should look, as did Ron and Brian, who basically drew New York. It must have been pretty confusing for the reader, seeing a different Mega-City each week."

Steve MacManus was pleased with his "discovery" of the vastly experienced Ron Smith because of what he brought to MC1: "He introduced a tremendous feeling for height to the city. He'd draw these dramatic aerial shots, you'd be looking down at the city miles below, that was really smart. His work has such a certain power and drive to it and he is so prolific, it made him quite a fixture." [See facing page].

Richard Burton agrees that the city is the key: "The Dredd stories are not about Judge Dredd, they're about Mega-City One. Dredd is a bit of a two-dimensional character – Dredd and Mega-City are almost a single entity."

MEGA CITY ONE
BY NIGHT

Whatever the problems in continuity, the early artists inspired those who followed in their wake, as Brendan McCarthy observes: "My style was heavily influenced by McMahon – a case of a first generation Dredd artist inspiring the next wave. Bolland was from a fine-art middle-class background, popular amongst the readers, while in stark contrast, Mike was the artists' favourite, he introduced an attitude of aggro, straight off the football terraces."

John Wagner leads many in judging McMahon and Bolland: "Of the early artists, I must say Mike and Brian were obviously the ones I liked drawing the stories. Mike would always bring something quirky to a story, always looking for something really different and exciting. I loved the quality of Brian's inking, it was so strong on the page it almost stood out in colours."

As well as continuity problems, the saga threw up another dilemma for Wagner to address. Judge Cal had reigned supreme, as Dredd's longest-running foe to date, but like the others he had died – killed in a death struggle with Fergee. So Wagner decided that killing off his main characters had to stop.

# DEATH BECOMES HER

In January 1980, *2000 AD* (Progs 149-151) unveiled the most important new villain since Rico – Judge Death, from the Death Dimension. The artistic creation of Brian Bolland, Death announced his arrival with a killing spree of unrivalled gore, plunging his skeletal claws deep into the breasts of his victims and tearing their hearts out.

Wagner's JUDGE DEATH three-parter could not have arrived at a better time. Three years into the existence of Dredd, fans were still waiting for an enemy who could stand up to him – up till now he'd blown them all away. As David Bishop points out: "The classic problem in Dredd has always been that he just turns up and shoots people – frequently to death. Introduce a great new character and Dredd just rides up and goes *'Bike cannon!'* and blows the guy to pieces. John had to come up with a new enemy week after week, year in year out – the Dredd strip just ate up ideas for breakfast. In JUDGE DEATH, here was an impervious enemy – at best he can only be contained. Death introduces the Moriarty to Dredd's Holmes."

Such was the quality of Wagner's creative characterisation, Death was not simply a cardboard horror freak, he had his own agenda – the creed that all crime is committed by the living, therefore life itself is illegal and must be destroyed. Not so much an anti-Christ, in the god-forsaken world of Mega-City One, Judge Death is the anti-Dredd, executing people in cold blood, but for all the wrong reasons.

Wagner had created an entity immune to Dredd's most powerful arsenal. If Death was the poison, Wagner needed an antidote. His solution was inspired – the beautiful PSI Judge Anderson, Dredd's psychic sidekick, whose vital powers are matched only by her vital statistics.

Although young readers, suddenly confronted by a powerful female in Dredd's male-dominated world, couldn't contain themselves over some aspects of the voluptuous Anderson, she at least could contain Judge Death and became host to him, sucking this evil incarnation into her brain. The Judges froze the pair in suspended animation to prevent him from escaping; importantly they did not – could not – kill him!

As well as Anderson, David Bishop also drooled over the artwork: "JUDGE DEATH features some excellent Bolland artwork although occasionally Anderson, who was supposed to have been based on new-wave pop diva Debbie Harry, sometimes looks more like Betty Boop."

> "Wagner's JUDGE DEATH was a masterstroke – at last here was an enemy Dredd couldn't kill. Already dead, Judge Death simply couldn't be terminated. He was genuinely scary, nasty and mysterious, he'd kill people in a graphic not bloody way and he would keep returning and returning..."
>
> DAVID BISHOP – MARCH 1995

Like Judge Death, Anderson became an instant hit with the fans. She also became a long-term fixture of *2000 AD*, achieving the accolade of starring in her own strip, which is still running today, although in some guises, Judge Cassandra Anderson looks more like her *Baywatch* namesake, Pamela. [See left]

Ironically Death brought new life to the strip and became as enduring as Dredd himself. Wagner is well aware of the importance of an indestructible nemesis in the development of Dredd: "At the time, I was looking for a formidable enemy. There was no prohibition on killing characters in *2000 AD* as there was in a lot of American comics of the time, where people would just get shot with stun bullets and survive to fight again. But in Dredd people did get killed, never to grace the pages again – until Judge Death, that is!"

Wagner liaised with Bolland over the visualisation of this evil new character: "I wanted Death to look like a walking corpse. I suggested that his uniform be a warped-version of Dredd's with details like the portcullis-type mask, a vulture instead of the eagle on Dredd's shoulder. But in cases like these, you just have to leave fine details to an artist of Brian's quality – he could never be tied down exactly to what you envisaged."

Bolland spent many a painstaking hour drawing the strip, but the lengthy gestation period was worthwhile and, to many in the business, JUDGE DEATH features some of his best ever work, as he confirms: "I was given the luxury of a couple of months to work on it but even then I don't think I finished on time, I never did! I took on the suggestions of Wagner and added my own – I might have come up with the pterodactyl thing on his shoulder and definitely the portcullis over his face, inspired by Kevin O'Neill's Torquemada character in *2000 AD*."

In just three episodes, Wagner had added two new and important levels to Dredd's world – the Death Dimension and the psychic Judges. As David Bishop observes, these innovations are somewhat wasted in three short episodes: "It's surprising that JUDGE DEATH is only a fifteen-page story, nowadays the temptation would be to spread it out for ever!"

Working on the theory that if you hit a winning formula, repeat it, only bigger and better, Wagner soon followed up with JUDGE DEATH LIVES (Progs 224-228), in which Death once more terrorises the citizens of MC1, but this time – ominously – in a more concerted effort, supported by three terrifying new allies from the Death Dimension – the Judges Fire, Fear and Mortis.

*[Right] This never before published drawing of Anderson was penned by Brian Bolland for a colleague.*

According to Richard Burton [one-time *2000 AD* editor]: "In the Four Dark Judges, Brian Bolland created four of the most evil and distinctive bad guys ever to appear in comics. JUDGE DEATH LIVES also features some of his very best work. The brilliant '*Gaze into the fist of Dredd!*' panel [see below] ranks as one of my all-time favourites. Very few artists can get that impact and raw energy into their work."

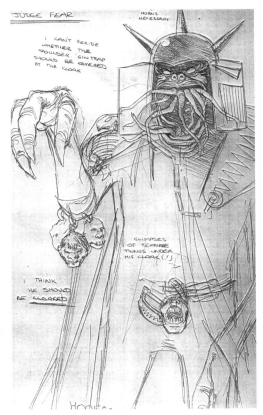

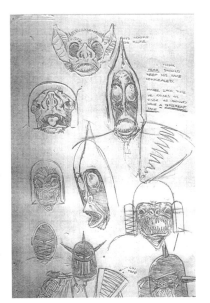

Bolland took his time creating the Four Dark Judges, producing endless preliminary sketches. But the wait was worth it. His recollection of the research process reveals how much thought goes into the creation of some Dredd characters: "When it came to JUDGE DEATH LIVES – they waited for ages for me to finish. I do recall that John sent me a number of photos and references for the Dark Judges, including one of an Australian Devil Fish. Sometimes I couldn't believe what John had been reading for research! He sent me so much background material that I ended up creating rough sketches for far too many looks for the Dark Judges."

Although Judge Death and his cohorts were eventually contained by Dredd, this vile ruler of the Death Dimension would be looking over Dredd's shoulder for years to come. Such was the potency of this poisonous creature, Wagner reintroduced Judge Death in many of his future strips, including, most importantly, NECROPOLIS and JUDGEMENT ON GOTHAM.

*[Above and far right] Four of Brian Bolland's previously unpublished rough sketches of the three Dark Judges Fear [above and top right], Fire [centre right] and Mortis [bottom right].*

*[Right] Death would always be at the back of Dredd's mind.*

# WHERE ANGELS FEAR TO DREDD

**THE JUDGE CHILD** (Progs 156 -181)
*Writers:* John Wagner and Alan Grant (from 177)
*Artists:* Ron Smith, Brian Bolland and Mike McMahon

> PLOT: A psychic PSI Judge predicts impending doom for Mega-City One – the saviour being a lost boy with the mark of an Eagle of Justice on his head. To find this saviour, Dredd undertakes an epic journey to the far corners of the Universe before finding and rejecting this "Judge Child" as an evil instigator of the deaths which occur.

After the heavy concentration on life in "The Big Meg", it was once again time for John Wagner to broaden Dredd out into the universe beyond. JUDGE CHILD is the third of the three great Dredd Mega-epics; like CURSED EARTH and JUDGE CAL, it is an event story which, as Richard Burton describes: "contains a significant development or event that affects the continuity of a whole series and the character therein. In JUDGE CHILD's case, it is Dredd's decision over the fate of the Judge Child himself."

More than this, the story marks the arrival of the most extreme grotesque parody yet seen in the Dredd strip, the crazy gang element as Dredd encounters increasingly surreal mutants, despots and kidnappers in his quest for the child. It works because Wagner had matured as a storyteller, adding a degree of economy to his epic-works. JUDGE CHILD is no rambling tale spreading across twenty-six episodes, it is served up to the reader in easily digestible two-to-three episode bursts, in which Dredd touches down in a new world, encounters its resident demagogue, discovers a new lead in his quest for the Judge Child and jets off.

Although considered by David Bishop to be a CURSED EARTH re-run, JUDGE CHILD, unlike its precursor, produced important new characters who found a place in the Dredd hall of fame and took starring roles in the Dredd movie – The Angel Gang (created by Mike McMahon) and, following the success of Anderson, a second female Judge – Hershey (created by Bolland).

Lessons had also been learned in the art department as a result of the JUDGE CAL debacle. Instead of seven artists, JUDGE CHILD was drawn by just three – McMahon, Bolland and Smith. This arrangement was closer to Wagner's ideal of two core artists and it produced some of their best-ever Judge Dredd work.

**Yet let me flap this bug with gilded wings**
**This painted child of dirt, that stinks and stings**

ALEXANDER POPE – EPISTLE TO DOCTOR ARBUTHNOT *(1735)*

*Richard Burton was mad about the boy: "THE JUDGE CHILD is one of the classic and longest Dredd Mega-Epics. It's memorable for so many things – Dredd among the planets, the first appearance of The Angel Gang, Bolland's eerie Jigsaw Man, and sub-plots that caused us nightmares for years afterwards."*

JUDGE CHILD demonstrates to those critical of allowing artists to do their own thing just how well differing styles can work, given the appropriate story. Ron Smith was happiest on large-scale crowd scenes into which he packed as many minute background characters as he could. This he demonstrated to effect in the episode TEMPLE OF THE GARBAGE GOD [see left], featuring Faro, leader of the Brotherhood of Trash, to Wagner's delight: "I liked the craziness of people like the Garbage God – Faro with his robe of ring-pull tabs."

But JUDGE CHILD is best remembered for ushering in the infamously violent Angel Gang, the wildest of Wild West characters ever created, whose delight in torture and murder make them a legend in the world of violent comics. The gang members are: Pa, Link, Junior and, the most maniacal of all, Mean Machine – with his limb-crushing robotic arm and penchant for head-butting frenzies. The Gang's attitude is best summed up by Junior: *"This sure is fun! I wanna kill an' kill an' never stop!"*

The Angel Gang [see right] were perfect characters for Mike McMahon to create, an artist happiest when drawing gritty, dark realism rather than clinical hi-tech subjects. As he recalls: "I saw them as Wild West characters – hillbillies, with a science fiction element thrown in with Mean Machine. Apart from him, the others were just thugs really! My instructions for Mean Machine from John were very specific – the dial on his head and a robotic metal arm with claw were both clearly detailed in the script instructions."

Wagner knew he had created sure-fire hit villains: "When I started the story I had a general picture of what would happen and I'd work things out as I'd go along. If you plotted it all out in advance it tended to become rather stale. The Angel Gang were quite spontaneous – I thought them up around about the episode they appeared. Mean Machine, in particular, was an obvious winner, one of those characters you knew was going to work."

Some of the exploits of the Angel Gang, particularly their glee in repeatedly torturing Old Joe Blind to death, is the stuff of which nightmares are made. But the readers loved it, and were only disgusted when the Angel Gang were ultimately killed off. Wagner believes that Ron Smith reached an artistic highpoint in the final three episodes on the Planet Xanadu where he finally disposes of the Gang in a serious of titanic struggles.

[Below] Disguised attractively as women, Link and Mean Machine face Dredd's firepower and 'Mean' develops his trademark lope-sided look.

If McMahon and Smith were in their respective elements creating and destroying the Angel Gang, Bolland's talents excelled when the story took off into the clinical sterility of spacecraft technology on board Justice 1. Here Bolland created a major new Dredd character in the female Judge Hershey. Like Anderson, Hershey is an all-too-rare powerful female presence in Dredd's world. She's not just another faceless, supporting character, but a strong, no-nonsense, physically capable Judge with attitude who puts Dredd down, repeatedly calling him Old Stone-Face.

The saga is best defined by the sudden change in pace into amusing cameo stories such as ALIEN TALE – a day in the love-life of a cave-painter, which John Wagner remembers with fondness: "I liked the Buggo story for linking Dredd to a God in the mind of these primitive savages."

Mike McMahon also cites this as his favourite part of JUDGE CHILD: "When a serial is going on and on it's nice to get a break. ALIEN TALE is completely self-contained – it had nothing to do with the real story. I was pleased with the artwork [see left], I'd got much more confident with my work towards the end of JUDGE CHILD. I felt I was doing the best work I could do at the time."

McMahon was also pleased with his episode featuring Sagbelly, the man-eating toad, and reveals that his fascination with the bizarre stems from a childhood experience [see right]: "My mum taught me to read using *Beezer* comic and I remember seeing a picture of hippopotamuses with their mouths wide-open, full of Japanese soldiers. It obviously had a terrible effect on me! I have more of an affinity with that kind of stuff. I wouldn't say that sci-fi is my forte, I'm much happier doing more naturalistic work."

IT
REAL
SE !

MY EYE JUST WENT! TH-THERE'S **GOT** TO BE A CURE! THEY'RE LYING TO ME! I'M AN ALIEN, SEE – THEY DON'T CARE WHETHER I LIVE OR DIE! IT'LL SAVE THE COST OF DEPORTATION IF I JUST **FADE AWAY**!

HING!

Once again writing to his artists' strengths, Wagner devised the surreal JIGSAW MAN especially for Brian Bolland [see left]. He was the perfect artist to draw the wasting jigsaw disease, with the ability to depict perfect geometry in his anatomical work – an area he sadly missed in constantly drawing the heavily-padded Dredd.

Despite all the comings and goings in outer space, Wagner was keen to reaffirm Dredd's personality. In THE CURSED EARTH, Dredd visibly softened in his approach and attitude to aliens and mutants alike. In JUDGE CHILD, even servo-robots felt an affinity with Dredd! [See right]

Although it saw the creation of some of the greatest Dredd villains, JUDGE CHILD also saw their immediate demise. According to David Bishop: "I know that Wagner always regretted killing off the Angel Gang [see below left] because they not only took over the story, they were the story. The best thing would have been to wound them or leave them out in deep space, then bring them back to Mega-City One – angry and wanting revenge. Instead they came up with Fink Angel, a long-lost member of the family who turned up looking for revenge."

THE WAY HE SPEAKS, GRUNWALDER! ALMOST LIKE A ROBOT HIMSELF!

I WILL BROOK **NO INTERFERENCE** WITH MY MISSION. ANY PERSON OR ROBOT WHO GETS IN MY WAY WILL BE **EXECUTED** UNDER SECTION 34b OF THE **SECURITY OF THE CITY** ACT. YOU HAVE BEEN FORMALLY **WARNED**.

YES! THERE IS **STEEL** BENEATH THAT FLESH. GIVE THE ORDER – HE IS NOT TO BE ATTACKED. I AM MOST INTERESTED TO SEE WHAT HAPPENS WHEN HE MEETS THE OTHER HUMANS . . .

THE FINK (Progs 193-196) is an example of a post-epic aftermath story. Drawn by Mike McMahon, who created the original Gang members, the poisonous Fink Angel [see right]– horribly mutated by Cursed Earth radiation – and his partner in grime, Ratty, seek murderous revenge for Dredd's annihilation of his family.

A final note in the importance of this saga – Part 22 is the point at which the John Wagner and Alan Grant writing partnership began. Grant had joined *2000 AD* in 1978 (on Prog 94), as sub-editor, before leaving to team up with Wagner to form what became one of the most enduring and productive writing partnerships in comics. Wagner's respect for his writing partner is clear: "He brought a lot to the story – he's fluent and imaginative with a good grip on what the readers want."

The new creative pair came together and, in their first full epic together, set about pulling Mega-City One asunder, which also led to the eventual loss of three key players in the history of Dredd...

I'LL KILL Y...

JUNIOR ANGEL: I FIND YOU GUILTY OF FOUL CRIMES TOO NUMEROUS TO MENTION. I SENTENCE YOU TO **DEATH**!

DREDD

THIS... CAN'T BE! I CAN'T DIE...

I'M HELL'S ANGEL

NEXT PROG: **LET JUSTICE BE DONE!**

ve] Dredd goes over the top. The end of
r Angel.

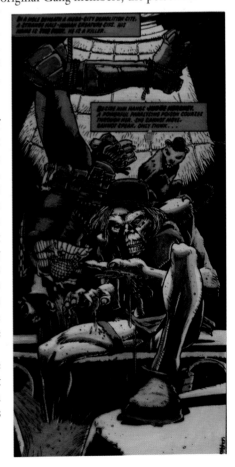

# WAR FOR WAR'S SAKE

**BLOCK MANIA** (Progs 236-244)
*Artists:* Mike McMahon, Ron Smith, Brian Bolland and Steve Dillon
*Writers:* John Wagner and Alan Grant

**THE APOCALYPSE WAR** (Progs 245-270)
*Artist:* Carlos Ezquerra
*Writers:* John Wagner and Alan Grant

*Joint plot:* Sov-Block city East-Meg One softens up Mega-City One for invasion, by sending in top Sov-agent Orlok to contaminate MC1 with a nerve-agent Blockmania – causing civil war.

The ensuing Apocalypse War – between the two Mega-Powers – sees MC1 repel all invaders and then destroy East-Meg One, but MC1's population is decimated with the loss of four hundred million citizens.

THE APOCALYPSE WAR is a tumultuous turning point in the history of Judge Dredd – the story and character. In an act of violent self-purging, the co-writers Wagner and Grant set about demolishing Mega-City One. The prologue story, BLOCK MANIA saw the artistic side self-imploding with the departure of definitive Dredd artists Brian Bolland and Mike McMahon, backed by the coming of age of a new generation – spearheaded by Steve Dillon.

The exit of the two main artists signalled the opportunity for the original Dredd artist, Carlos Ezquerra, to make the first of his dramatic comebacks. As well as the city, and the artists, the writers also sacrificed yet another major character – Dredd's heroic stalwart Judge Giant.

For Wagner and Grant, this purging of the strip was a major act of artistic bloodletting. Through their visual interpretation, the artists had overpopulated MC1, and the city had grown out of control, it was no longer a realistic or manageable concept. Now the writers wanted to claim back their heritage, so they decided to rip it up and start again. This act of creative sabotage was the necessary culmination of urban tensions seen in – BLOCK WAR (Prog 182) and the Grant/Gosnell scripted THE AGGRO DOME (Prog 183), while the chosen source of the destruction – the Sov-city of East-Meg One – had been hinted at in BATTLE OF THE BLACK ATLANTIC (Progs 128-129).

In many ways, the tasty hors d'oeuvre of BLOCK MANIA is more satisfying than THE APOCALYPSE WAR main course – an all-out, shoot 'em up which pulverised the readers for six months.

The Sov-agent of destruction, Orlok almost manages to rival Rico, Judge Death and the Angel Gang in the memorable villain stakes: "Orlok's a rarity," says David Bishop, "a Dredd villain who survives." Through the services of Orlok the writers commit the equivalent of comic-strip suicide. Judge Giant's untimely death at the hands of Orlok is remembered by many as one of the all-time great comic let-downs. In a realistic but downbeat way he is simply shot in the back, as Wagner freely admits: "Sorry, folks. Had we the chance to write it all again we'd give him a death worthy of Hamlet." [See right]

"Wagner and Grant wanted to destroy Mega-City One – starting with a civil war in BLOCK MANIA and culminating in THE APOCALYPSE WAR."
*MIKE McMAHON – APRIL 1995*

"Mega-City One was getting too big. We'd seen other writers and artists extend its borders as far south as Florida, north into Canada and west practically halfway to the Rockies. It was no longer a manageable concept. It was time, we decided to whittle MC1 down to size."
*JOHN WAGNER AND ALAN GRANT – JULY 1984*

[Below] Having previously only drawn one Dredd strip ALONE IN THE CROWD (Prog 205), Steve Dillon had the task of disposing of a Dredd legend: "I was given the honour of drawing this major point in Dredd's history – the death of Judge Giant, who in effect was Dredd's best mate."

MORE NEXT PROG.

David Bishop is quick to agree: "Giant was just thrown away! They didn't make a big thing about killing the character which you would do today – hype it to death. Judge Giant was such a great character, vaguely cool, a little bit hip, Dredd had a professional respect for him – something which made him seem almost human."

As well as the passing of Giant, comic fans also mourned the departure of two giants of art – Mike McMahon and Brian Bolland – from the strip. McMahon painfully recalls that the very act of pruning the city, in BLOCK MANIA, necessitated drastic action and dramatic visuals: "This meant masses of crowd scenes, and it took me four weeks to draw the first episode. I enjoyed doing it but it was just too time consuming – you just couldn't make a living like that." Ironically, McMahon believes that this first episode of BLOCK MANIA [see below right], his penultimate work on the strip, features his best-ever artwork on Dredd: "I really got into my stride then – visualising the costumes they wear, making it a lot more realistic. It was a supreme story focussing on the absurdities of the lives of the ordinary people in the Mega-City – the horrible lives they lead rather than any huge science-fiction epics."

McMahon continues: "For the second episode [see below] I just bluffed it and then bowed out. I could just see myself going bankrupt!" Scheduled to draw all nine episodes, he gracefully bowed out after the first two, with Smith, Dillon and Bolland re-assigned to take over. McMahon's

conscientiousness had taken its toll.

Meanwhile, Brian Bolland, his time increasingly taken up with demands for his talents in America, and frustrated at becoming bogged-down in over-detailed work on Dredd, left to work for DC Comics. As he remembers: "I'd started to have doubts and became disillusioned with my work. I was taking so long to finish everything and was becoming very late with my work. Mike and I both felt it was time for a change. We didn't want to become solely identified with one comic character, we needed to leave Dredd. I had found that I'd almost lost the ability to draw simple human anatomy – elbows, knees, shoulders (as intimated with the Jigsaw Man from JUDGE CHILD). With Dredd, everything was covered up by those huge pads and you never got to see any detail in his face."

Bolland's departure to the USA, together with that of close friend and fellow *2000 AD* artist Dave Gibbons, heralded a fast-flowing stream of UK creative talent, writers as well as artists. Bolland symbolically announced his arrival on the front cover of the American comic – *Amazing Heroes* [see right].

This artistic drift Stateside would threaten the very foundations of *2000 AD* in years to come – the comic soon becoming the victim of its own success. The fact that Dredd was the number one strip in the comic guaranteed that editors would only commission the cream of British artists to work on it – and they were the first to go.

From 1982, American comics publishers, divining this new pool of British talent, started attending UK comics conventions and began to offer artists and writers not only excellent page rates, but royalties – something previously unheard of in British comics. Dredd was the pinnacle for comic artists in Britain, the next step up was the States – the home of the comics they'd grown up reading and idolising.

With Bolland and McMahon gone, Carlos Ezquerra was back in what he felt was his rightful place as the number one Dredd artist. Having visually conceived Judge Dredd back in 1976, he had finally come to terms with his disappointment at not being the first Dredd artist to be published. As Steve MacManus puts it: "Carlos had overcome his problem on Dredd. He is not happy to share his work on a strip, as had been the practice on Dredd. Now he was back doing what he liked best – drawing a six-month war epic on his own."

Never before had a Dredd epic been completed by just one artist. Ezquerra had come back from the cold after five years away from the strip. THE APOCALYPSE WAR wasn't just a *new* beginning for Carlos, it was quite simply the beginning – the real start of Ezquerra's Dredd career.

"Only Carlos could have had handled THE APOCALYPSE WAR," says Steve MacManus, "Twenty-five episodes, week in week out – it was a tremendous achievement. His experience of working on war comics obviously helped him – he was in his element drawing the tanks and bombings of the war in the streets of Mega-City One, it was a great example of sustained artwork." [See following three spreads]

After THE APOCALYPSE WAR, Dredd had shown himself to be the reader's ideal of a comic strip hero – although this view may have gone against the grain Wagner (and Pat Mills) had originally planned for him. But the readers were to have their own say in how Dredd would ultimately develop as a character.

Over the next couple of years, Wagner was happy to let Dredd drift through a sequence of light-hearted stories typified by titles such as THE LEAGUE OF FATTIES (Progs 273-274), BOB & CAROL & TED & RINGO (Progs 346-349) and REQUIEM FOR A HEAVYWEIGHT (Progs 331-334) – the last of which saw Carlos Ezquerra's final Dredd strip for six years (until KIRBY'S DEMON – Prog 638).

Following these two years of fairly insignificant fun stories which gave little progression to Dredd's development, Steve MacManus remembers a significantly serious turning point: "At every convention we went to the readers would complain that Judge Dredd was perfect and never had any doubts. After listening to this for years John and Alan agreed to do a story where he has doubts. If you speak to Wagner he'll say that it was wrong to do that."

Back in 1984, under pressure from the readers, Wagner and Grant first added major elements of Dredd's self-doubt and fallibility in the trilogy QUESTION OF JUDGEMENT, ERROR OF JUDGEMENT and CASE FOR TREATMENT (Progs 387-389). Although this humanisation may have pleased the readers, Wagner himself was unhappy with the development: "It was an experiment but I didn't like it. As I've often said, I am very afraid of altering his character at all. I've always been wary of having Judge Dredd change too much – if you change a character you're in danger of losing it altogether. DC don't change Batman – he may be portrayed as the Dark Knight – but he's still your essential Batman."

In QUESTION OF JUDGEMENT, Dredd voices his regret for killing an armed murderer fleeing the scene of his crime, when he could have simply detained him. He confesses his guilt to Judge Morphy, an old-timer who, as Dredd's former rookie supervisor, continues to act as his mentor...[See left]

In the following story, ERROR OF JUDGEMENT, Dredd takes pity on a girl, Bonnie Crickley, who is psychologically unbalanced, after her brain has been transplanted into an ugly robot body following an accident. In an uncharacteristic display of compassion, Dredd flouts the rules and arranges for the government to pay for her treatment.

"Dredd really does screw up big time, [see below]" says Alan McKenzie. "He takes pity on a kid, he tries to help her, but it goes horribly wrong [the girl throws herself in front of a truck] – it would have been better if he'd left well alone in the first place."

As a result of misusing official funds, Dredd himself becomes a CASE FOR TREATMENT, which focusses on his fitness and state of mind to carry out his job. Under hypnosis Dredd regresses to his early years as a Judge. Although the doctor can find no psychological cause for Dredd's problems, no apparent guilt for Rico's corruption or death. The marked contrast between the young, tunnel-vision Judge and the Dredd in his present, doubt-ridden state is inescapable. [See below]

Having been forced down a creative cul-de-sac, expressing the dark side of Dredd's persona, Wagner and Grant decided it was time to re-establish the youthful, rebellious, free-spirited side of the comic strip.

# BRUSH UP YOUR SHAKESPEARE

*"Chopper exposed the repression of Mega-City One and shone brightly as the spirit of youthful rebellion."*

*JOHN WAGNER – MARCH 1995*

Marlon Chopper Shakespeare first appeared in UNAMERICAN GRAFFITI (Progs 206-207), as a dare-devil graffiti artist [see right]. In an inauspicious debut, he was just another punk, like the earlier "Spikes" Harvey Rotten, who appeared in MEGA-CITY 5000 and was reborn in THE CURSED EARTH.

What set Chopper apart was the fact that he survived – Chopper is a kid and the law of comics decreed that children cannot be terminated. With Chopper, Dredd was on to a loser from the very outset.

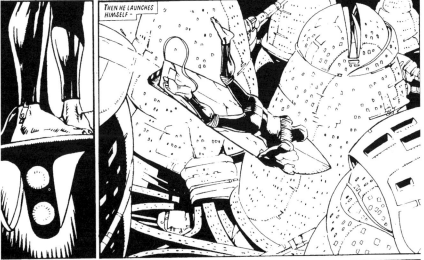

Here was a fly on the wall that he could not swat, the readers loved him – like them Chopper was young and rebellious, he struck an immediate chord. At last Dredd faced an opponent with whom they could identify.

And not just the readers: "Chopper remains one of my favourites of all the Dredd supporting characters," admits Richard Burton, "He is a free spirit in a structured, regimented world. I vividly recall, not long after this story, a rash of real Chopper graffiti appeared around London – even in the train I took to work each morning! I remember feeling both elated and disturbed at the influence *2000 AD* was having on society."

The character which Chopper transformed into in MIDNIGHT SURFER propelled him into the league of superstar status [see left]. He became a renegade surfer, a free spirit joyriding on flying surf-boards, dicing with death as he raced around the Mega-City One skyline. He was cool, he could fly, but above all he could beat Judge Dredd – without the need for violence.

Beautifully told over six breathtaking episodes MIDNIGHT SURFER tells the story of Chopper's bid to win Supersurf 7, and become the champion power board surfer of the world.

The reappearance of Chopper stands as one of the most popular stories ever to grace *2000 AD* and is one of John Wagner's personal highlights: "In story terms MIDNIGHT SURFER is one my all-time favourites. Chopper was the good guy who really exposed Judge Dredd as being a real bad guy. It was something we should have done a lot earlier, but we didn't have many heroes apart from Judge Dredd. They tended to appear and get killed, whereas Chopper was one that actually stayed around."

Steve MacManus found another element which makes it one of the most nail-biting of Dredd stories: "The beauty of the story is that Dredd is on to Chopper from the start. In effect, MIDNIGHT SURFER is about two races: Supersurf 7 and Chopper's own race to beat the law. In fact if ever a Dredd story made you root for the lawman's quarry – this is it."

It is also helped by the brilliant art of Cam Kennedy, who, as Richard Burton feels: "Really made you think a sport like this could exist and that there was a little bit of the Silver Surfer in all of us." Burton is hinting at the obvious inspiration for the story, Marvel Comics' Silver Surfer originated by Stan Lee and Jack Kirby in 1966.

Kennedy employed his own distinctive technique in developing the character, created by Ron Smith four years earlier: "I was given Ron's version as reference for the story, which of course I immediately ignored! John gave me a lot of scope and a very free hand to interpret what he had written. I saw Chopper as the kind of spiky-haired kid you might see in a 1950s American war movie, clean-cut, running up the beaches of Iwo Jima – I just made his hair a bit longer. He was a really free spirit, a kid who knew he was surrounded by all these Judges, yet he had this passion to surf which completely dominated his life. He knew the risks he was taking but off he went. That's why the ending's really nice, people appreciate that he flies down and saves the life of his Japanese opponent, even one of the Judges next to Judge Dredd says '*Is that surfing or is that surfing?*' Of course Dredd says, '*Surfing, schmurfing he's going down*' – completely emotionless as always."

David Bishop selects MIDNIGHT SURFER as one of the definitive Dredd stories: "In UNAMERICAN GRAFFITI, he'd been fairly mediocre, now he's liberated as a character, thanks to dynamic visuals and a damn good story. Chopper would dominate Judge Dredd matters for many years."

Just as the writers had been guided by the voice of their readers, so Dredd was to be influenced by the democratic voice of Mega-City One – the people. Just as Chopper had shown MC1 the ways of freedom and self-expression, so Wagner and Grant would build on this over the next six years. Combined with Dredd's growing doubts about his own origins, the strip would now follow a crucial course that would inextricably lead to the total destruction of Mega-City One, the Judge System and Judge Dredd.

# LITERAL DEMOCRATS

"To a degree the democracy and doubts storylines are separate strands, but they gradually become more and more entwined as the strip leads to Dredd's resignation."

*DAVID BISHOP – APRIL 1995*

DEMOCRACY IS A CANCER EATING AT THE HEART OF OUR SOCIETY. ANY ACTION WE HAVE TO TAKE TO STAMP IT OUT – HOWEVER REGRETTABLE – IS JUSTIFIED.

With the benefit of hindsight, the politicising of Dredd was inevitable. What could be more of an anathema to Dredd's original fascistic police-state than a return to Democracy? The last great test of the all-powerful Judge System lay in its ability to prove itself in the face of a greater power – that of the people.

Hitherto, no other system of government or law enforcement had been considered in the strip. The original concept still held good – a mega-city of chaos, over-populated by criminals, mutants, crazies and weirdos, there being only one law – the Judges. In this environment the power of the ballot was never a serious alternative to the power of the bullet (all six options).

Entwined with Dredd's increasing doubts over his own lineage and role in life, the writers introduced a fundamental questioning of the role of the Mega-City rulers. The first hint of democracy came as early as LETTER FROM A DEMOCRAT (Prog 460) [see right].

This one-off story features freedom fighters calling for the overturn of the tyrannical Judges: "This democracy storyline obviously gave political depth to Judge Dredd, assessing how fascist his society is and that makes it a crucial story – the politicising of Dredd," says David Bishop.

Some sixteen months later, Wagner and Grant returned to this germ of a democratic idea in REVOLUTION (Progs 531-533).

Sixteen million citizens marched for democracy [see left], but the movement had been infiltrated by the Judges. The march self-imploded resulting in mass arrest. John Higgins, who drew REVOLUTION, admired the story for its political satire, believing it revealed Dredd, the authoritarian, stamping on the power of the people, in the harshest light ever [see below].

In their next epic, the writers combined the strands of doubt and the dark element of Dredd's ancestry, temporarily ignoring the growing democracy strand, taking Dredd down-under.

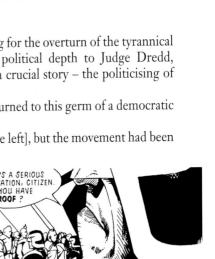

THEN LET THIS BE A LESSON TO YOU, CITIZEN. DEMOCRACY'S NOT FOR THE PEOPLE.

THIS IS YOUR DOING. YOU SET IT ALL UP!

THAT'S A SERIOUS ACCUSATION, CITIZEN. DO YOU HAVE PROOF?

I DON'T NEED PROOF! YOU'RE JUDGES, AREN'T YOU? YOU LIE AND CHEAT AND CONNIVE – YOU DO ANYTHING TO HANG ONTO YOUR PRECIOUS POWER.

ANY ACTION WE TAKE TO STAMP OUT PERNICIOUS IDEAS LIKE DEMOCRACY IS JUSTIFIED – FOR THE GOOD OF THE PEOPLE.

DON'T MAKE ME LAUGH! WHAT DO YOU KNOW ABOUT WHAT'S GOOD FOR THE PEOPLE?

DOING THINGS YOUR WAY? DOING WHAT WE'RE TOLD? FOLLOWING ORDERS? LIVING IN FEAR ALL OUR LIVES?

TAKE HER AWAY!

# OZMOSIS

Covering another twenty-six episodes, OZ provides a sharper than ever focus on Judge Dredd's parentage. As Richard Burton announced, OZ is a sequel to the immensely successful MIDNIGHT SURFER and the ever-popular Chopper – who escapes custody to participate in the world power-board championships down-under. In pursuing the ever-elusive Chopper, Dredd has a much more important axe to grind – to save Mega-City One from "himself".

Wagner and Grant originally planned OZ to be drawn by MIDNIGHT SURFER's Cam Kennedy and the equally inspirational Brendan McCarthy – whose working vacation to Australia inspired his creation of a new dynasty of Dredd characters, the Judda and the Oz Judges (including the Pythonesque Judge Bruce). Kennedy had to decline the series, due to his commitment to DC Comics, and his workload was passed onto seven other artists – Cliff Robinson, Jim Baikie, Garry Leach, Will Simpson, Steve Dillon, Barry Kitson and John Higgins.

*"Ostensibly OZ is MIDNIGHT SURFER goes antipodean - of course, with Wagner, it's much more than that."*
RICHARD BURTON - APRIL 1995

As far back as THE RETURN OF RICO (Prog 30) it was revealed that Dredd was a clone of the Judge System, but no clue as to his actual parentage was ever established. Ten years later, OZ reveals that his genetic father was Fargo, the first Chief Judge of Mega-City One, who had died many years before Dredd popped his head out of the test tube.

Fargo had "appeared" in previous stories such as the JUDGE CAL saga, which showed his tomb complete with its Father of Justice inscription – although at that stage, the "father" of Dredd had not been contemplated by the writers. This genetic link was more specifically referred to in DREDD ANGEL (Progs 377-383), in which Fargo and other heroic figures of MC1 are singled out as donors of perfect Judge-making DNA – but still no direct link to Dredd.

Since Wagner had gone back into the depths of Dredd's backstory to create his heritage, he was bound by some salient pointers – Dredd's cloned twin Rico had been impure and turned against the Judge System. This dark side of Dredd, and more importantly of Fargo, was something Wagner (with Grant) built upon with devastating results over the ensuing years.

Although the writers may not have decided upon the Fargo-Dredd link until many years after RICO and JUDGE CAL, one theme that runs through the years of Dredd is his constant battle against himself - in the guise of Dredd clones (RICO), Dredd robots (CAL), Dredd ghosts (CITY OF THE DAMNED - Progs 393-406) and Dredd doubles. Even the fact that many of his worst enemies have been Judges is a theme that runs through Dredd's very psyche, since he subconsciously cannot come to terms with his creation.

Harking back to the much earlier 'Yellowknife' strip in *Valiant* (see page 11), Wagner has always used the dual device of pitting the hero against his double. This theme continued with Dredd - and never more vividly than CITY OF THE DAMNED [see left].

Just as Pat Mills had done in THE RETURN OF RICO, now Wagner and Grant felt it was their turn to send in the clones.

In OZ, Dredd discovers that one of the evil Judda (Judge killers), came from the same Fargo DNA as himself. This meant that the unseen killer, referred to as Simeon, was another Dredd twin. This sets in motion Dredd's journey to the Ayers Rock headquarters of the Judda, his mission to destroy these evil clones, where he confronts the founder of the Judda – Morton Judd, the former head of genetics at Mega-City One, in the days of Fargo.

A typically evil scientist, Judd tried to assassinate Fargo and his fellow Judges to replace them with his own brand of docile, cloned Judges. With his master-plan foiled, Judd escaped to Oz, taking with him stolen supplies of the valuable DNA. There he cloned a whole tribe of evil Dredds who were intended to invade Mega-City One and overthrow the Judge System. As the head of his private army of Judges, from the same élite but flawed stock as Dredd, Judd was the most serious threat to Mega-City One since the Sov-Cit Judges in THE APOCALYPSE WAR.

OZ reaches a climax when Dredd confronts Morton Judd and discovers the scientist is not so much his father as midwife to his own family of evil Dredd clones [see left and below]. Dredd eventually destroys the Judda and the Ayers Rock HQ, but the story leaves a loose end, as not all the Judda in Mega-City One have been accounted for. The writers had carefully planted a time bomb – ticking...ticking...ticking...

During OZ, one bombshell that did explode was the break up of the very successful but fraught writing partnership of Wagner and Grant, as the

latter describes: "As we worked on OZ, it became quite clear that our mutual vision of Dredd and his world was starting to diverge. In particular, John wanted to bring a stronger feeling of realism into the story and to show Dredd still had a human side; I favoured taking the strip even further into grotesque parody."

Matters came to a head between the writers as they tried to plot Chopper's fate in the final episode. As the two heatedly discussed their different endings, Wagner pointed out to his partner just how much time these diverging views were costing them, which Grant plainly states as: "John always liked Chopper. My own feeling was simple – Dredd should kill him." Wagner won the day with Dredd being distracted while trying to shoot Chopper out the sky, so Chopper made good his escape. [See right]

Their destructive double-vision irreconcilably blurred, the co-writers completed their last *2000 AD* work together on Dredd. If Dredd's bloodline was crucial, the decision not to kill off Chopper was equally significant. Chopper had become a metaphor in the Dredd canon. Once more he had evaded Dredd and won his race – he was not an arch-criminal out to destroy MC1, but, for all his skill and experience, Dredd could not nail him and it exposed fatalistic failings in Dredd's professional pride.

Wagner ensured Chopper's survival not, as Grant intimated, because he liked the character, but because it engendered Dredd's guilt over his failure, and neatly picked up the thread of self-doubt which Wagner had already been weaving into the story.

Although credited to both writers, the story that immediately carried on the OZ plot, THE HITMAN (Progs 571-573), was written solely by Wagner, and as Grant observes: "It mirrored Wagner's changing ideas about Dredd's development – ideas which were calculated to usher in the most dramatic upheaval since Dredd's inception."

In THE HITMAN [see right], a haggard and hospitalised Dredd, critically wounded by a Judge killer, worries about his actions. Above all else, he is haunted by his failure to kill Chopper. This is the human side of Dredd, which Wagner wanted to develop – not the compassionate side but the dark, brooding side of regret and guilt.

Two months and just four stories later, Wagner delicately detonated another contributory factor governing Dredd's fate. The time-bomb that had been left ticking at the end of OZ exploded in BLOODLINE (Progs 583-584). The only Judda left alive in Mega-City One, after the failed invasion, took his first faltering steps to becoming a replacement for Dredd – whose DNA dynastics he shared.

# BLOOD IS THICKER THAN WAGNER

> "Kraken could never replace Dredd, he was an even heavier character, he was too contaminated."
>
> *JOHN WAGNER – APRIL 1995*

Where OZ had hinted at the possibility of a rival clone posing a threat to Dredd, in BLOODLINE that threat became a reality. The story reveals that the only Judda to have escaped the bad day at Ayers Rock had been spared by Chief Judge Silver, who felt he could rid the clone of Fargo's dark-side and use him to good effect in MC1.

This clone-prince of darkness was called Kraken. He shared Dredd's lineage and, more importantly, he was younger, fitter and unburdened by years of toil on the streets which were grinding Dredd down. The dual-personality BLOODLINE is symbolically told over two episodes, with the clones meeting [see left], then going their separate ways – but they'd meet again.

Pat Mills, who created the definitive clone concept in THE RETURN OF RICO, remains protective of his original idea: "If John had re-cycled my Rico character, I would have been very defensive about the story. But since he chose to use a new clone and his writing came from the heart, I was quite happy for him to continue the thread of what I had started all those years before."

Where Mills had created his clone concept around a relatively youthful Dredd, Wagner was dealing with a battle-hardened and bruised veteran [see right]. Alan McKenzie (former editor) explains the ageing process: "The saga of Mega-City One unfolds at the same pace as real life unfolds. Every year that goes by Dredd gets a year older – unlike Spiderman, who has been a university student for the past twenty-five years!"

Kraken would not reappear until a year after BLOODLINE, when he would take a leading role in Dredd's unfolding tragedy. In the meanwhile, Wagner continued to submerge himself in the ageing process in intervening stories such as IN THE BATH (Prog 626) [see below].

IN THE BATH's artist Jim Baikie recalls: "I liked the way John explored Dredd's realisation that he was getting old. At the time, John was talking to me about his ideas for a story where Dredd goes out into the desert and thinks about his future – to be TALE OF THE DEAD MAN."

Dredd's age became a major debate during this period with fans and staff worried about the problems associated with a character who was becoming increasingly decrepit with each passing year. Yet Dredd's physical ageing remains strangely incongruous given the availability of advanced medical technology in Mega-City One – the power to rejuvenate the elderly and genetic face-changes (introduced in THE NEW YOU – Prog 2). Old Stoney Face could easily have been given a make-over without losing credibility. He had already benefitted from medical science – after his eyes had been plucked out by a robot in CITY OF THE DAMNED, he was fitted with a pair of bionic replacements.

But were Dredd's advancing years also a sign that John Wagner was himself becoming a little weary of writing the character? Many observers, including the *2000 AD* editorial staff, hold the view that Wagner was ready to quit writing Dredd; that, after a dozen years, he had grown tired of his creation and wanted to kill Dredd off – destroying all his handiwork. This apparent act of hara-kiri could also be explained by Wagner's growing anger at the continued lack of royalty payments for his creation.

Wagner today cannot recall his exact thoughts about Dredd during the late 1980s. When asked if he had become tired of Dredd at this time, Wagner does concede that he became "intermittently weary of it, although I would have been immediately revitalised after writing a few good stories".

Wagner denies that he wanted to quit writing the strip, adding that he might have toyed with the idea of introducing a lighter Judge Dredd "in the sense of a Dredd no longer burdened by worries and doubts".

In the end he did change his mind, realising that to change Dredd's personality, to give him more depth of character, as often demanded by editors and fans alike, would destroy the Dredd mythos altogether.

Mid-1990 saw Wagner revitalised after a year and half penning his more favoured, lighter-hearted short stories, including a number of historic strips: BAT MUGGER (Prog 585 – Wagner's first Batman-inspired strip); TWISTER (Progs 588-591 – Wagner's homage to *The Wizard of Oz*, which saw the Dredd strip finally go all-colour) [see left]; OUR MAN IN HONDO (Progs 608-611 – the debut of major Dredd artist Colin MacNeil, who would link up with Wagner for their masterpiece AMERICA), and KIRBY'S DEMON (Prog 638 – the return of co-creator Ezquerra to Dredd after six years).

With his batteries recharged, Wagner was about to set Dredd his stiffest test yet. The 3-D dimensions of Doubt, Democracy and DNA were about to strike at the very heart of Dredd. Wagner was preparing to take Dredd to the brink of self-destruction and launched into a serial of high-fibre proportions with a little Snap, Kraken and Pop!

# A PAEAN IN THE NECROPOLIS

> "NECROPOLIS laid to rest five years of development, it was going to be John's grand finale. He wanted to destroy everything he'd built up and then leave. But he changed his mind."
>
> *DAVID BISHOP – FEBRUARY 1995*

NECROPOLIS (Progs 674-699) may have been five years in Wagner's cooking pot – with a pinch of Doubt here, a measure of Democracy there, and a dash of DNA seasoning, but what he served up fed *2000 AD* readers for a whole year.

Starting in October 1989 with Kraken's return in THE SHOOTING MATCH (Prog 650), Wagner's feast ran through such courses as A LETTER TO JUDGE DREDD (Prog 661) where Dredd's doubts on democracy come to a head; TALE OF A DEAD MAN (Progs 662-668 – which followed on the *2000 AD* series 'The Dead Man') where Dredd fails "near-perfect" Kraken as a rookie, and takes the Long Walk deserting MC1, and BY LETHAL INJECTION (Progs 669-670) where Chief Judge Silver "executes" Kraken but secretly revives him to take Dredd's place.

These stories were all written by Wagner to set up his ultimate nightmare scenario NECROPOLIS – another twenty-six part epic, which he admits took several months to work out because of all the intricacies of the complex plot: back tracking, adding new layers and re-thinking the storyline. This need for immense backstory coupled with his dislike of epics may explain Wagner's choice for such a dark saga.

Over the years, Wagner had found himself increasingly under pressure to come up with bigger and better epics. Not an easy task given the past reader appreciation for the likes of THE CURSED EARTH and OZ. Editorially, Wagner and Richard Burton knew that every two years or so, it was time to launch into another mega-epic.

Burton recalls that NECROPOLIS could well have grown out of this pressure in which Wagner suggested writing Dredd's epitaph. Both Burton and Wagner admit that the notion of killing off Fleetway's most lucrative character would never have been sanctioned. That is not to suggest that such possibilities were never discussed, as Burton is quick to point out: "Many seemingly far-fetched ideas are bandied about in the creative process. It's a case of thinking up the most extreme or crazy ideas and then work back from that point. NECROPOLIS was such a case." The pair just happened to start with the notion of killing the Golden Goose-stepper.

As suggested, Wagner laid the foundations to his next epic through a carefully constructed series of introductory stories, each having their own "event" which fired the final saga into action.

In TALE OF A DEAD MAN [see above right], Dredd reacts more like a drowning man, as his past life, his doubts and despair flash before him. He vividly remembers the letter sent to him by a schoolboy (in LETTER TO JUDGE DREDD) which innocently revealed all that was wrong in Dredd's society – the inability of the Judges to contain crime and the death of law-abiding citizens, whose only crime was to ask for the return of their civil rights in the massive Democracy march.

Also in TALE OF A DEAD MAN, Dredd again comes face to face with his nemesis when he is chosen to street-test the rookie Kraken [see right].

In a tragically ironic twist, Judge Morphy, Dredd's mentor in QUESTION OF JUDGEMENT, is gunned down and Dredd finally cracks. The symbolic death of his pseudo-father figure is too much for Dredd, when confronted by another twin from the same genetic father. Dredd fails Kraken, even though he performs faultlessly on the streets and disposes of a group of Democratic freedom fighters with consummate ease – reminiscent of Dredd as a trigger-happy, cocksure, young Judge.

The turning point of the story comes when Kraken contemptuously denounces Dredd: "Your time's over old man." This arrogant put-down convinces Dredd that the Judda is not dead – merely resting in Kraken. He also realises that as a Fargo offspring, he himself must have a dark side.

With doubts about his bloodline and democracy now at their most destructive, Dredd does not stay to fight Kraken. He leaves, taking the traditional Long Walk (albeit on his Lawmaster) to oblivion, signifying a Judge's usefulness in MC1 has come to an end. [See right]

His face burnt away by the corrosive acid of the Cursed Earth, Dredd, no longer resplendent in his uniform, is just another mutant. He had become the Dead Man, and NECROPOLIS spelt Death – in many guises – for Dredd and Mega-City One. [See left]

Wagner knew that to bring Dredd back credibly, from his never-ending journey to the centre of the Cursed Earth, would require the services of his ultimate enemy – Judge Death.

With Dredd's alter-ego Kraken now secretly ensconced by Chief Judge Silver in his role as the Mega-City's number one crime-fighter, the four Dark Judges return [see right] and turn MC1 into the City of the Dead. The Sisters of Death, a terrible triumvirate from Death's Dark Dimension, exploit Kraken's suppressed hate and turn him against his city. Dredd finally returns and, with the help of Judge Anderson, seizes back control, but not before sixty million citizens have perished.

In NECROPOLIS, Wagner had taken Dredd halfway to damnation and back. Kraken had proved to be too bad to replace him and Dredd had returned because only he and Anderson were capable of disposing of Judge Death and his cohorts.

Dredd had faced his future head-on [see left] in the form of his identical twin, Kraken, in a scene highly reminiscent of Dredd confronting Rico. Again, having overcome yet another self-test, Dredd looked at his double, found it wanting and without hesitation blew his twin away.

Like THE APOCALYPSE WAR, NECROPOLIS was planned as a blood-letting war to end all wars. Wagner had once more intended to level the city he had so effectively populated and with it, destroy Dredd – this old, doubting warrior, who had seemingly taken the Long Walk into interminable oblivion. The Dredd that emerged post-NECROPOLIS was re-born, and not just because his acid-ravaged face had been rejuvenated. The epic was not a case of Wagner starting out to destroy Dredd and pulling back, leaving the character in limbo. As Steve MacManus believes: "Dredd emerged from the story invigorated. By allowing him to take the Long Walk all the bad air had been released and new life had been breathed into the character, he had been de-coked."

Having killed off his personal doubts and his evil twin, Dredd was ready to face his last great test of character – the voice of Democracy.

# THE BALLOT OF JOHN AND YOUR CALL

Having sown the first Democratic seeds in QUESTION and ERROR OF JUDGEMENT, seven years earlier, this final flowering of Dredd's 3-D vision came to full bloom with Wagner's swansong strip in *2000 AD* – THE DEVIL YOU KNOW (Progs 750-753).

Having put the readers' and successive editors' minds at rest on Dredd's doubts about his genealogy, Wagner knew he still had to supply the finishing touches to the question of Dredd's doubts over Democracy. Wagner's farewell trilogy showed that the post-NECROPOLIS Dredd had recovered from his depths of despair and doubt to such an extent that he was willing to test the integrity of his hallowed Judge System.

THE DEVIL YOU KNOW [see below] placed Dredd in grave personal danger from his peers, who were prepared to kill him, since Dredd now openly championed the citizens' call for a referendum to decide between a return to Democracy or to stay with the much criticised Judge System.

> "The democracy series grew out of my own internal struggle with the character of Dredd. I disagree with much of what he does and I'm always tempted to move Mega-City One towards democracy, although I always pull it back. But it is the direction in which it's going."
>
> *JOHN WAGNER – APRIL 1995*

Dredd's own political stance had never wavered, he was demonstrably against Democracy, but he did have lingering doubts about his own conduct in smashing up the protest march in REVOLUTION.

The people of Mega-City One had acknowledged their great debt to the Judges by erecting the Statue of Judgement. Dredd now sought their support again and was prepared to gamble the future of the Judge System, in a re-affirmation of his own beliefs and in justification of his role.

In the follow-up story, TWILIGHT'S LAST GLEAMING (Progs 754-756 – written by Garth Ennis, under the direction of Wagner), the referendum went 68% in favour of the Judges. Two million unhappy Democrats marched on the Great Hall of Justice, but Dredd quelled the riot as he plainly spelt out the bitter truth to Blondel Dupre, leader of the Democrats. [See below]

As far as *2000 AD* was concerned, the cathartic denouement of the democracy series was John Wagner's last gleaming – THE DEVIL YOU KNOW was to be his last original Dredd strip for *2000 AD* for almost four years. Having made his final on-page protest against the running of affairs in MC1, he was set to make his own protest in the long-running battle of creative royalties. As Pat Mills revealed earlier in this book, Wagner's chosen method of protest was normally to give up and walk away, but the reborn Wagner was about to silence his own doubts and exercise his own form of democracy. He was now ready to take his own Long Walk.

This Mega-history has so far concentrated on Dredd's development as a character and a comic strip, and touched on the creative forces and their battles fought behind the scenes to get certain elements included in the strip. To fully understand the second creative struggle, off the page – not only in Dredd and *2000 AD*, but in all British comics at the time, it is necessary to put two of these episodes into context with the Dredd strip.

In 1986, an important, embittered episode in *2000 AD*'s history culminated in the supposed celebrations of the comic's 500th issue. Due to a lack of royalty payments for their input and their overall treatment by the publishers, there was not only die-hard dissention amongst the *2000 AD* artists and writers, there was mutiny at the very pinnacle. Steve MacManus, editor since 1978, set the ball rolling...

# FATAL ART ATTACK

In the now infamous 500th issue, internal dissatisfaction came to a head in a series of bitingly satirical diatribes entitled THARGSHEAD REVISITED – which Pat Mills, creator of *2000 AD*, describes as "the most self-criticising thing that the comic had ever done".

Steve MacManus had called on Mills to organise the storyline which was a visit inside Tharg's brain [Tharg being the "editorial voice" of *2000 AD*] – with the contributors and their characters (including Dredd, Halo Jones, Dan Dare and Torquemada). Mills remembers "arranging the stories with loving care to appear wildly critical of IPC management including John Sanders".

In retrospect the attempt to mount such a politically motivated protest through a comic owned by such a large corporation as IPC, was a little naive and one quickly quelled by management, who pulled two strips – by Brian Bolland and Mike McMahon – from the printing presses.

Mills angrily recalls the controversy surrounding Bolland's offering (published here in this form for the first time): "John Sanders rang me up at eight o'clock one morning and was absolutely livid. He pulled Brian's artwork just before it went to the printer and he killed the most crucial story of the five – Brian's celebrated Dredd clown. It was along the lines of '*Try and merchandise Dredd now*'. None of the creators was getting a slice of Dredd merchandise. It was witty and very funny, a real classic."

This never before published photo-copy from his THARGSHEAD strip is all that Bolland has of his original, long since missing from Fleetway offices (along with over a hundred other pieces of original artwork). Mocking the Dredd merchandise which earned no reward for the writers or artists, Bolland sent up all his most beloved creations – most cruelly and memorably Dredd himself.

The strip was finally published (in the *1988 Judge Dredd Annual*) in a much censored form – Bolland's own words being toned down and the frame of Tharg on a toasting fork removed.

Mills also remembers McMahon's banned strip 'Bloodsuckers' (also reproduced on the facing page for the first time with McMahon's own original lettering): "Mike was being heavily plagiarised by other Dredd artists, whose names even I refuse to mention, and he was obviously very upset about it. He wasn't making any money and all these guys were copying him – blatantly tracing his artwork."

Again the IPC censor struck and McMahon was forced to recreate a sanitised page, but recalls his original attack on the 'swipers' who were stealing his art: "I must admit it was done half in fun, half in anger.

> "THARGSHEAD REVISITED **reflected all our bitterness on the exploitation of the comic and the fact that none of us was being properly rewarded. It was full of venom, I saw it as a catharsis for many of the people involved and a lot else besides."**
>
> *PAT MILLS – FEBRUARY 1995*

"I don't mind people copying my style, it's just when people take traces off my pictures! For example, it took me weeks to draw BLOCK MANIA, if someone wanted to draw an episode like that by tracing it, they could have done it in an afternoon – and get the same money. What disappointed me most was the staff who worked for *2000 AD* should have known and told them not to do it. I just think that if you aspire to be any good as an artist, you don't go around blatantly ripping off other people's work!"

[Left and below] Homage or swipe? Compare these two pieces of Dredd artwork to McMahon's original masterpiece on page 80.

After almost ten years of Dredd, the creative team of artists and writers had tried to voice their dissatisfaction in the only way they knew how – through their work. But it had fallen on deaf ears. It would take new management to finally listen to their demands, but THARGSHEAD importantly signalled the start of the battle for a new deal.

# YOU'LL NEVER WALK ALONE

> "So we bought a pack of cigarettes
> and Mrs Wagner pies,
> And we walked off to look for America."
>
> *PAUL SIMON – AMERICA (1972).*

In 1990, three years after THARGSHEAD REVISITED had tested the water, and at much the same time as Dredd was taking the Long Walk, John Wagner decided to take his own Long Walk over the fight for royalties. With no cards left up his sleeve to play, Wagner declared misère in a gamble that would have impressed the real T. B. Grover – and took the Long Walk...into potential oblivion and fronted the front man.

Newly appointed Fleetway managing director Jon Davidge (who had replaced John Sanders – a couple of years after Maxwell Communications bought Fleetway from IPC) vividly recalls being forced to play the Wizard to Wagner's Dorothy after his Long Walk down the Yellow Brick Road to his office: "I had only been at Fleetway for a week or two when John Wagner paid me a visit. To show how new I was to the job I didn't originally know who John was. He turned up in my office with a suitcase and proceeded to empty this suitcase full of Judge Dredd merchandise onto my desk. He looked at me and asked, in his gruff Scottish voice, *'You know I created Dredd? Well, guess how much I've made on all these?'*

"I explained to him that I hadn't had a chance to read his contract, so I didn't know. He quickly brought me up to date: *'Not a fucking penny!'*

"John threatened never to write for the comic again, unless I sorted out the royalty payments. He also warned me that all the other writers and artists would do the same.

"Coming from a book publishing background, I was used to paying creator's royalties, and was truly surprised that the contributors had no down-the-route income. I didn't consider it at all fair and agreed to make some far-reaching and very necessary changes.

"I didn't change the way we rewarded people for first publication rights – since we were competing for the top people, we paid the best rate in the UK anyway. So, I agreed to pay a 50% creator's royalty on all secondary use, by our definition almost a gross profit, which I'm happy to share equally. It's a perfectly fair deal all round."

The result of Wagner's Last Stand would not only benefit the writer and Carlos Ezquerra as credited co-creators of Dredd; any writer or artist who created other characters in Dredd's world would also benefit. Four years after their plaintive protest in THARGSHEAD REVISITED, the creatives' interests had been recognised – in monetary terms.

David Bishop reflects on the impact of Wagner's Long Walk into Jon Davidge's office: "Up to then Fleetway had never paid anybody any royalties for anything – now we do. We were haemorrhaging good writers and artists, who used *2000 AD* as a stepping stone and went off to work in America where they could make royalties.

"Nowadays you can make money working for Fleetway beyond the page-rate. So Mike McMahon who co-created the Angel Gang and Mean Machine [in JUDGE CHILD] which appear in the Dredd film and merchandise will make some money out of them. After all those years of having his artwork swiped, all those hundreds of thousands of Titan albums sold, the T-shirts, the pyjamas, everything, Mike and others in his position have been given a fair deal."

Having taken one of his now legendary walks when *2000 AD* was first published, back in 1977, John Wagner was keen to be at the helm during the launch of Fleetway's latest comic launch *Judge Dredd: The Megazine*. This new publication was another positive knock-on effect from Wagner's stand and was seen by Fleetway as a way of harnessing Dredd's expanding universe and cast of strong, supporting characters.

Wagner and Alan Grant moved over to launch *The Megazine* as consultant editors, developing stories and writing many of the strips for the initial issues working with managing editor, Steve MacManus. But in contrast to his situation when *2000 AD* was launched, Wagner now had a financial stake in *The Megazine* beyond just the standard page rate, as David Bishop confirms: "With its launch, John's loyalty visibly shifted from *2000 AD* to *The Megazine* and has stayed with it ever since. He's built up a hardcore loyalty with it and, more importantly to him, he's got a royalty deal. He makes money on every issue sold, so he cares more about the title than he ever did about *2000 AD*.

"I could never understand why he suddenly became so ambivalent toward *2000 AD*, until I read an early draft of this book and learned for the first time about the failed buy-out of *2000 AD* by Pat and John. *The Megazine* is to a very large degree Wagner's baby and he was very keen to make sure it grew up properly."

Since the first *Megazine* was published in 1990, until the start of 1995, Wagner only had twelve original Dredd strips published in *2000 AD* – his final story being THE DEVIL YOU KNOW (Progs 750-753 – 19 October 1991). At that time, Wagner kept himself busy concentrating on writing the perfect opening strip for his new publication, which David Bishop simply describes as "the best Judge Dredd story ever written!"

When asked to name *his* favourite Dredd story out of the hundreds he has written, John Wagner has no hesitation: "Obviously AMERICA. I was very happy with that, I thought it really worked well as a story. It exemplified things that I felt deeply about the Judges. In a way it was a true tragedy – people were compelled by their own character into disasters."

David Bishop elaborates on his superlative opening salvo: "My first choice from *The Megazine* has got to be AMERICA. It's the citizen's eye-view of what it's like to grow up in Mega-City One [see right]. It's ultimately a love story and it says an awful lot about the DEMOCRACY storyline."

This personal summary succinctly introduces the basic plot: Born of immigrant stock, America (Ami) Jara grows up to become disillusioned with life in Mega-City One, and she spurns the love of a childhood friend to join the outlawed democratic rebel faction Total War. After a series of

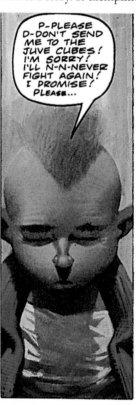

terrorist attacks and Judge killings, Ami is finally betrayed, and shot dead in the shadows of the twin Statues of Liberty and Judgement.

But, with the magical touch of a master mortician, Wagner manages to extract life from death in two simple yet shatteringly effective final twists, which Bishop remembers as being chilling and deeply political: "It's got that incredible twist in the final episode. Just when you think it's a bitter-sweet, happy ending, you turn over the page – and there's one more page. It's Dredd effectively kicking you in the teeth, saying 'forget about it, there's no such thing as democracy, people can't be trusted' and it's really restating the case for a total police state."

Bishop doesn't reserve all the accolades solely for Wagner's story: "Colin MacNeil produced the best example of painted art of any Dredd story – before or since. The strip brought out the best in everybody involved and was instantly hailed as a classic. It was so mature, and it showed that you can do a deep and meaningful Judge Dredd story."

Quite rightly, MacNeil also regards this strip as his favourite piece of Dredd art, and it is the story when he felt his art came into its own: "I'm peace-loving by nature and I wanted to show the violence graphically, to show violence for what it is, so the reader would feel '*Look what happened to him. I wouldn't want it to happen to me*'."

Despite the purported purity of his painting, the artist owns up to a crucial piece of time-saving: "The final pics of the Statue of Liberty are actually a photocopy taken from a children's book on New York, which I painted over. In the later stages, I found the artwork was taking three times as long as normal, because it was so difficult, so detailed and because I loved it so much. I usually manage a page a day, but AMERICA took me two to three days per page."

The seven-part story also served to cement the new comic's credibility, as Bishop explains: "AMERICA immediately pitched *The Megazine* as being older than *2000 AD*, and clearly defined its separate identity. The story also heavily influenced all that followed in the title, developing into a maturer title."

*[Left] Despite the mature message contained in AMERICA, Wagner still managed to permeate proceedings with his brand of media-inspired humour, again backed to the hilt by MacNeil's astonishing art – all of which served to give a new slant to Dredd's draconian devotion to the law.*
*This excerpt also underlines the feeling that Dredd was a direct descendant of the Wild West marshals who sought to clean up the lawless frontier towns.*

Bishop's final words on AMERICA reveal further aspects of Wagner's craft: "John has got a massive emotional stake in the story and you get the impression he had to put himself through the wringer to write it. There's a lot of personal stuff in there that John will never tell anyone about. We've frequently talked about a sequel – although, every year, when he mentions a follow-up, I know he'd have to put himself through hell and back in order to write it, to match the first one. I also know Colin MacNeil would crawl over broken glass to paint it!"

*ART NOTE*: The inside front and back covers of this book are taken from the opening two pages of AMERICA. These twin peaks of perfection symbolically set the tone for the emotional episodes awaiting the reader and amply sum up Dredd's (and quite probably John Wagner's) single-minded resolve.

# ANYONE FOR ENNIS?

**"If Judge Dredd is written badly, he can get away with it because he still looks cool. In the last few years, some of the stories not written by John or Alan are appalling – but it doesn't mattter so much because John's and Carlos's original creation is still there – the world still looks cool. So even if the story's awful, there's always the chance that John will come back and write the next one."**

*PAT MILLS – MARCH 1995*

Unfortunately for *2000 AD*, after THE DEVIL YOU KNOW, John Wagner chose to concentrate on his writing and new found editorial duties on *The Megazine* (and other non-Dredd writing projects). To cover for his abdication, he chose a successor to lead Dredd's *2000 AD* readers to the promised land.

DEATH AID (Progs 711-715) marked the first Dredd script to be written by Garth Ennis, who recalls his debut: "In the summer of 1990, John liked my work in *Crisis* and *The Megazine*, and asked me to do a few fill-in stories on Dredd because he was getting snowed under writing for *2000 AD*, *The Megazine* [in particular AMERICA], and for the USA. Up to then, John had been writing Dredd on his own for two years, after Alan Grant had left during OZ. As it turned out, after a few fill-in stories, I took over full-time on Dredd in *2000 AD* for the next couple of years."

EMERALD ISLE, an early Garth Ennis's fill-in strip inspired by his roots, spawned one of the most famous pics in recent Dredd history [see right], as the writer recalls: "That poster pic by Steve Dillon was my idea. I had decided, since other countries had their own Judges, Ireland should have theirs, but different. Dredd was a total action man, dedicated to his job – a brutal killing machine. I didn't see that for the Emerald Isle Judges – who were more like regular cops, who did their nine-to-five shift and then went down the pub for a Guinness."

During the next couple of years, in which he wrote the bulk of the Dredd stories for *2000 AD*, Ennis's main claim to fame is the monster, mega-epic JUDGEMENT DAY (Progs 786-799 and *Megazine*). This twenty-part blockbuster broke new ground for Dredd in that the story was published simultaneously in both *2000 AD* (14 parts) and *The Megazine* (6 parts).

Despite its length the plot is easily explained in three sentences:

Earth is threatened by its dead rising and killing the living.

Judges from the surviving Mega-Cities meet in Hondo City (Japan), put aside their petty differences and agree to nuke a number of overrun Mega-Cities (including MC2) to halt the zombies.

Dredd, along with a select band of Judges and Johnny Alpha, defeats the evil necromancer Sabbat, and save what's left of planet Earth.

Wagner had groomed Ennis from the start for one last mega-epic, which Richard Burton gladly relives: "The Biggie! Sub-plots from several different stories were pulled together to form a mega-saga of epic proportions. It was one of the most challenging Dredd stories I can remember working on.

RIP Mega-City Two – it looked like a nice place to live!"

Although solely scripted by Ennis, this story is co-credited to Ennis and Wagner, but Ennis has his own take on this: "The sum total of John's collaboration was that we decided Dredd needed a mega-epic to end all epics, with a big, big threat – and John felt zombies were the order of the day.

"Basically, I decided that we needed to up the ante over previous sagas, which explains the imminent destruction of Earth and not just Mega-City One, as in past episodes [see right].

"I also wrote in a number of new characters as well as weaving in friends and foes from Dredd's past. The most exciting of these was Johnny Alpha (from *2000 AD*'s 'Strontium Dog'), included to give the readers extra interest. It also gave Carlos Ezquerra the chance to pair up his legendary visual creations Dredd and Alpha in some unforgettable scenes, including the final frame of the saga." [See facing page]

Ennis also resurrected Murd the oppressor from the JUDGE CHILD saga to act as Sabbat's trainer, and included a welcome return for Judge Hershey.

Having been in control for a couple of years, Ennis developed his own view on Dredd: "I really do like him – he can always be relied on to do the same thing every time. He never shifts from enforcing the law, and he'll shoot anyone at the drop of a piece of litter. I didn't grow up reading him...but he's the sort of character that never changes – still the same old bastard, so it doesn't really matter which period you grew up reading.

"Although he always responds in the same way, he is a little more sophisticated than a one-note character – he definitely has a style of his own, but really that's getting beyond the whole point of the strip."

*TRIVIA NOTE: The epic nature of the saga is heightened by the fact that this is the first time the world's Judges act together as one unit.*

Ennis's mentor John Wagner confirms the promise he first saw: "Garth is a really good writer – he could be very big, not just in comics. I think he was struggling under a weight of years of Wagner and Grant when he took over from us – it was an impossible task. He ended up in a way mimicing us rather than bringing Garth Ennis into the story."

Not everyone connected with the comic(s) was so diplomatic about the Ennis era. David Bishop feels this period marked the nadir of *2000 AD*'s Dredd strip: "Under Garth's scripting, it went well for six months, then he got bogged down doing other work and Dredd ceased to be the focus of his time. Some of the stories were really just making up the numbers and I'm sure Garth would be the first to acknowledge that.

"Then, other writers came in on Dredd and *2000 AD*, and the focus was lost for the next three to four years – it wandered lost through the first half of the 1990s, because John wasn't writing it.

"There's nothing that stands out in *2000 AD* once you get past NECROPOLIS. For me the back-to-back stories THE DEVIL YOU KNOW and TWILIGHT'S LAST GLEAMING (which were about a year on from NECROPOLIS), was the last great hurrah – that was it, that wrapped up the last elements of DEMOCRACY.

"After this we had JUDGEMENT DAY but that's a story that created more problems than it resolved because we killed almost the entire supporting cast of Dredd. This was a blatant failure to learn the lessons from Judge Giant's death in BLOCK MANIA."

This wouldn't be the only lesson that those on *2000 AD* would learn...

# A COMEDY OF ERAS

The final lesson that all concerned on *2000 AD* learned was that reading a Judge Dredd strip not written by John Wagner was like listening to *My Way* not sung by Frank Sinatra. Whatever new versions may appear, there is only one Judge Dredd, and there is only one Dredd writer, as his peers are quick to make clear.

Artist Ron Smith draws first blood: "Wagner was a bloody genius! Because he had edited *Lion*, he knew all about comic-strip characters, but when he created Dredd he threw the rule-book away! Heroes are supposed to have that cool grin. Here was Dredd – his face never revealed – with that down-turned mouth."

Former Editor Richard Burton pays tribute to Wagner's longevity: "I don't think there's anybody I admire more as a comic writer than John. In terms of consistency, how many other writers would create a character nearly twenty years ago and still be able to come up with fresh, original ideas all these years later? Dredd's success is down to John alone. His imagination and professionalism is so there and so rare in this business. I have total admiration for the man's body of work – which is just incredible. John does the job – which is the greatest accolade you can give someone in comics. They do the job – and do it well."

Alan McKenzie follows his predecessor's line: "Nobody is in the same league as John – he *is* Judge Dredd. He is the quintessential British comics writer, he excels in six-page chunks. Whereas many comics writers these days are inspired by other comics, Wagner writes from life. That's his trick, art imitates life, life doesn't imitate art and that's why Wagner's work has so much truth about it – truth with a capital T."

Perennial co-writer Grant gives a further insight into their joint writing style: "For inspiration, John and I used to look through the newspapers for interesting headlines that we could turn into Dredd storylines. For instance, if we read that a Conservative MP had been caught in a spanking sensation, we'd write a Dredd story about spanking. We may not always have had something to say, but we used to try and parody current affairs that the readers could relate to."

> "John Wagner had much more to do with setting Judge Dredd in his ways. Dredd is an extreme extrapolation of John's own disciplined character."
>
> *ALAN GRANT – JANUARY 1995*

[Right] Whistle while you smirk! The captions and dialogue from these frames illustrate Wagner's style, as an excerpt from Arkensword fanzine suggests: "What sets John's writing apart from others is his biting satire. It may be funny at first glance, but it can be chilling the next."

TRIVIA NOTE: THE ART OF KENNY WHO? [below] took its title from an editorial conversation with an American publisher, who was asked about using the artwork of Dredd artist [Cam] Kennedy, and he replied: "The art of Kenny who?" Kennedy actually drew this strip and based the title character on himself.

Having written hundreds of Dredd scripts with Alan Grant, Wagner also examines their relationship: "We are quite similar, we've known each other since our days at D.C. Thomson – we definitely work best as a duo with comedy. It's an awful lot easier to write comedy, you feed off each other with comedy. In a way, we've given a comedic bent to most of the stuff we've done. If you look at our Dredd stories very few are absolutely deadpan. We also like writing about obsessions and the absurd. They're more fun to write and more satisfying than the normal, straight-action adventures."

As Wagner suggests, he is far happier with the comedy aspect of Dredd, but he always manages to include vouchsafed references with a deeply serious, political comment – as shown by JUDGE DREDD AND THE SEVEN DWARVES (Judge Dredd Annual 1987). [See above]

Two further examples of Wagner's wonderfully warped humour laced with biting satire and social comment are unveiled by Alan McKenzie:

"I liked THE ART OF KENNY WHO? (Progs 477-479) for two reasons – one because of the reprise of the timeless Abbott and Costello routine [Who's On First – see left] – really funny. But underneath this humour Wagner hits a home-run, because the Kenny Who character is a comic strip artist who sends his art samples to a publisher, who programmes his samples into a computer to duplicate his style, so Kenny never gets paid. The cynical of us here would say isn't that what happened to Jack Kirby – everybody copied his style? Dredd is at its best when it's making you laugh but making a serious point at the same time."

McKenzie continues: "THE BIG ITCH [*Judge Dredd Annual 1983*, see below] is about superfleas from the Cursed Earth, which bite everybody causing a terrible frenzied itching, driving the citizens to suicide and causing traffic accidents. The dialogue is pure Dredd – such a Wagner comment."

Having intimated previously that Dredd without Wagner is like Wise without Morecambe, or Ridgeley without Michael – the two go hand in hand – David Bishop expands upon his premise: "Having let other people write Dredd, John discovered that no one else can write Dredd as well as he can, because he created it. Other people only seem able to grasp the superficial elements of Dredd, they can't really grasp the core of the character, which to a degree is a warped version of John, a distillation of certain elements of John himself."

Two stories that best demonstrate Wagner's complete mastery of Dredd are BURY MY KNEE AT WOUNDED HEART (*Megazine* 46) and the graphic novel JUDGEMENT ON GOTHAM written three years previous, at much the same time as AMERICA.

BURY MY KNEE AT WOUNDED HEART marks Wagner's belated return to form on his favoured strip, as David Bishop emotionally relates: "I burst into tears reading the script when it first came in, it delivers such an emotional kick – those first two pages slay you utterly."

After AMERICA, this one-shot story was clearly David Bishop's next best Dredd episode, as it marked the return to the true Dredd spirit: "The mail we got on this one story was just incredible – because everybody had been fed a diet of mediocre Dredd stories for about three years. Since the end of the DEMOCRACY series, the strip had turned into *Terminator*/Arnie shoot 'em up stuff, but KNEE suddenly evoked Dredd's human side. He was still a bastard, but it didn't mean he was utterly without compassion.

"To a degree, it shows Dredd can be human enough to make the right choice every now and then – it changed the readers' perception of the character again.

"John wrote a beautiful story around an awful pun that he'd been dying to use for years. But he was worried the title would cheapen the story – you've got to accept that not everyone has heard of the book about massacring Indians."

Bishop continues: "The story is about a couple, both aged a hundred and twenty-two, who've been married for ninety-one years, and survived together through the Atomic Wars, the Apocalypse Wars, Necropolis, Judgement Day – everything. The wife dies in her sleep, after her husband has promised he'll bury her, like the old days, she won't be just sent down the conveyer belt at Resyk. But, he's not rich enough to bury her, so he hires a robot, and breaks into a cemetery to illegally bury her. Dredd catches him [see right] and takes him off to see his wife's body going through Resyk. John didn't know how to end the story, but found a truly poignant yet typically Dredd-like finale [see below], in which he reveals he, himself, has a heart."

*TRIVIA NOTE: Wagner actually returned to 2000 AD (Prog 919 – 23 December 1994) with a ten-part Dredd story EXTERMINATOR, which he'd originally written some years earlier, for DARK HORSE, inspired ironically by the Terminator movie. But this storyline had been rejected and Wagner, some years later, customised his script for Dredd – for his return to 2000 AD and Dredd.*

Bishop's final words on this story: "John enjoyed the positive response and, about that time, *2000 AD* persuaded him to come back just to write for a year on Judge Dredd to coincide with the release of the Dredd movie, around Prog 950. So after a break of some three years, he's back writing in both *2000 AD* and *The Megazine.*"

# BAT TO THE FUTURE

Some four years before the Sylvester Stallone film became a reality, the sustained success of Judge Dredd was finally confirmed when he teamed up with another crime-fighting legend, who himself had recently been Hollywoodised.

In 1991, after fourteen years, Dredd eventually came of age with his elevation to the world league of comic strip legends, when he was paired with DC Comics' number one crime-fighter – Batman [see right] – in the graphic novel JUDGEMENT ON GOTHAM. Worldwide sales in excess of 400,000 copies stands as a solid testament to Dredd's arrival and acceptance on the international scene.

The sixty-four page story was again co-written by Wagner and Grant – the latter having already written Batman stories for DC Comics. To give this historic episode in Dredd's development greater meaning, the writers included key characters from his past – villains Judge Death and Mean Machine, and fellow MC1 Judge Anderson. From Batman's stable of villains came The Scarecrow, who neatly counterpointed Dredd's nemesis Judge in the boo-hissss ssstakes.

Wagner's inclusion as writer harked back to an earlier Dredd meeting a Bat-figure in BAT MUGGER (Prog 585, 30 July 1988), which had been a dress rehearsal for the proposed graphic novel tie-in, three years later. Drawn by Batman artist Alan Davis, who used Wagner's spoof Batman script (including Judges Gordon and Robin, and City Blocks Wayne and Grayson) to acquaint himself with the Dredd figure [see below right]. But various factors conspired to delay the Lawman-Batman union and Davis was fated not to draw Dredd's coming of age.

This honour fell to Simon Bisley, who was riding the crest of the new-wave of comic art following his 'Slaine' series for *2000 AD*: "I would class it as a good career move, it gave me the chance to do Dredd and Batman, which gave me the exposure to display my wares in the States."

*Animal writes movement - the Bat goes eye-ball to eye-ball with the Eagle.*

Within the sixty-four pages, Bisley managed to capture the quirky qualities of the support cast. But it was the titular twosome who created most problems: "It wasn't a very difficult job, but – working for Fleetway and DC simultaneously – it was important to give an equal billing to Dredd and Batman on the cover…[see overleaf]

DREDD